IN REPLY REFER TO:

AG 201 Whipps, Ernest R.
PC-N ETO 102

20 April 1945

Mrs. Ida Whipps
493 Maynard Avenue East
Columbus, Ohio

Dear Mrs. Whipps:

This letter is to confirm my recent telegram in which you were regretfully informed that your son, Staff Sergeant Ernest R. Whipps, 35,293,631, has been reported missing in action in Germany since 1 April 1945.

I realize the distress caused by failure to receive more information or details; therefore, I wish to assure you that in the event additional information is received at any time, it will be transmitted to you without delay. If no information is received in the meantime, I will communicate with you again three months from the date of this letter.

Inquiries relative to allowances, effects and allotments should be addressed to the agencies indicated in the inclosed Bulletin of Information.

Permit me to extend to you my heartfelt sympathy during this period of uncertainty.

Sincerely yours,

J. A. ULIO
Major General
The Adjutant General.

1 Inclosure
Bulletin of Information

'TIL WE MEET AGAIN

A MEMOIR OF LOVE AND WAR

RAY & BETTY WHIPPS
WITH CRAIG BORLASE

Tyndale House Publishers, Inc., Carol Stream, Illinois

Visit Tyndale online at www.tyndale.com.

TYNDALE and Tyndale's quill logo are registered trademarks of Tyndale House Publishers, Inc.

'Til We Meet Again: A Memoir of Love and War

Designed by Ron Kaufmann

Edited by Stephanie Rische

Published in association with the literary agency of D.C. Jacobson & Associates LLC, an Author Management Company. www.dcjacobson.com.

Scripture quotations are taken from the *Holy Bible*, King James Version.

Library of Congress Cataloging-in-Publication Data

Whipps, Ray, date.
    'Til we meet again : a memoir of love and war / Ray and Betty Whipps, with Craig Borlase.
        pages cm
    Includes bibliographical references.
    ISBN 978-1-4964-0548-7 (sc)
1. Whipps, Ray, date. 2. Whipps, Betty. 3. World War, 1939-1945—Personal narratives, American. 4. World War, 1939-1945—Prisoners and prisons, German. 5. Soldiers—United States—Biography. 6. Prisoners of war—United States—Biography. 7. Married people—United States—Biography. 8. Christians—United States—Biography. I. Whipps, Betty. II. Borlase, Craig III. Title.
    D811.W448 2015
    940.54'7243092273—dc23
    [B]   2015010154

Printed in the United States of America

21   20   19   18   17   16   15
 7   6   5   4   3   2   1

We will have been married for seventy years on September 29, 2015.
We have seven children plus their spouses,
nineteen grandchildren, and thirteen great-grandchildren.
We dedicate this book to God, who brought us together,
and to our families, who have been so loving to us. —*Ray and Betty*

To Don Jacobson, the best-looking Yoda I've ever met. —*Craig*

Contents

Preface

GETTING OUT OF BED IS NOT EASY this morning. It hasn't
been easy for years. My heart isn't what it used to be, my
hand's still a little stiff, and my knees seem to ache more
and more each time I get up. But today I don't want to
stay here a moment longer than I have to. So I push and
pull until I manage to break free from the sheets that have
curled themselves around me. The nightmare is over, but
the raw emotions still linger at the edges of my mind.
I look over at the other side of the bed and see that it's
empty. *She must be awake already*, I think.

I need to get up.

It was the same dream I've had countless times in the
past seven decades. There are men beside me, and they're
my men. It's my duty to keep them safe, to keep them alive.
There are Germans up ahead, a full squad of them—maybe
two or three of them for every one of us. I know two things
in the dream: that we are outnumbered, and that I have to
get my men back alive.

Even though in the dream I know I am young and fast and strong, as soon as the first bullet zips past my head, I feel my limbs suddenly turning to stone. It takes everything in me to put one foot in front of the other and to call out to the men as I fire on the enemy.

I'm not aware of what's happening to the Germans, and I don't feel particularly scared or troubled. What I mostly feel is the mighty responsibility of these young men's lives. If I don't do my job right, their deaths will be on me.

So I have no choice but to press on and fire my rifle until the Germans turn and run. The harder I fight, the louder it gets. The clamor of rifles, machine guns, and grenades gets so loud that I think it's going to deafen me, until finally the Germans retreat. The dream is over.

This is not the only dream I have, and it is not the worst. There have been other dreams over the years—dreams where I have watched, frozen, as men died next to me. Those dreams are the worst, and I'm thankful they don't come around much anymore.

Even so, this nightmare was bad enough to make my body feel a little hollowed out. I close the bedroom door behind me and walk down to the kitchen. I stand at the sink as I wait for the coffee—a morning ritual I've come to rely upon these past few years.

My eyes move across the room, reading the story it tells. I study the photos that crowd the refrigerator door—an endless sea of bright faces belonging to children, grandchildren, and great-grandchildren. I smile at the crayon pictures that are pinned to the wall, a series of princesses and robots and rather abstract animals. There's also a picture of Betty and me, taken at a wedding one summer not too long ago. *This is a good story*, I tell myself.

I'm careful to pour the coffee over the sink so I won't spill on the counter. I take the half-full cup over to my chair, where I can reach for my Bible. When I close my eyes to pray, I can still feel the dream. I keep my eyes open.

These days this is about the worst of it. It was so much harder when I first came back from the war. All it took was the sound of a revving engine and I'd jump for cover. Every year when the Fourth of July approached, I felt a knot of anticipation growing inside me. I thought I'd left the war behind, but it followed me all six thousand miles home.

Even so, I never went through this alone. I've never gone through any of this alone.

I hear a noise outside and turn to watch the door slide open. And there she is—my Betty. The only woman I've ever loved.

"Good morning, Ray." Her smile hasn't dimmed one bit in the seventy years since I first saw it. "You had a rough night?"

"A little," I say. "But not so bad. Did I kick you?"

"Yeah. But not so bad."

"You know, there can't be too many ninety-four-year-olds who swim every morning and walk a mile each way to get there."

She just shrugs in that way she does, smirking a little at me. "I don't want to get fat," she says with a grin.

"Oh, Betty." I smile back at her.

Betty settles in to the chair next to mine, and I pull out my Bible. We have so much to be thankful for.

1

TOO NIMBLE TO DIE

I LAY STRETCHED OUT on the limbs of a beech tree so solid I believed that even a tornado couldn't shake it. Unlike the tree, though, I was small and light. Years later I would be glad that my thin frame and light bones made me quick on my feet, able to scramble out of harm's way. But back then, all I knew was that while most of my friends would have thought twice about climbing quite so high, I had no fear of going as far and as fast as possible.

My parents' home was four houses away, but this tree—standing in the middle of a small strip of land between the end of the street and the railway line beyond—was mine. At least that's what I said to the bare branches that filtered out the sunlight. The tree and I were made for each other, and nobody knew the routes up or down the way I did.

It was a sunny winter afternoon in the final days of 1929, and even though the tree was bare, I knew I was almost invisible. Below me, the afternoon carried on as usual. In the distance, streetcars unloaded and restocked their human cargo, ferrying them in and out of downtown Columbus, a five-cent ride away. Every once in a while, trains passed on one of the two parallel lines that ran through town.

Though it had been a month since the start of the Great Depression, I was almost totally unaware of what was going on in the world. For the eight-year-old me, perched above the street, everything was just as it was supposed to be. I lay back and stared at the sky beyond the branches.

There was a breeze, but nothing like the kind of wind that sometimes blew through my Ohio hometown. On those gusty days, my friends and I would fashion paper and sticks into kites and then attach secret messages to the tails before releasing them to the skies. We'd let the winds take them higher and higher, eating up the string that unleashed from our hands until the kites were barely visible. When we'd had enough of watching the bird-sized dots wrestle in the wind, we'd begin the long task of reeling them back in. Finally, with arms and hands aching, we'd examine our downed kites, eager to see which messages had been taken by the clouds.

Lying on the thick boughs of the beech, I thought about the skies. But that day I wasn't thinking about kites; I was contemplating a different sort of flying. *What would it be like to be a fighter pilot?* I wondered. *How would it feel to sit above the battle, waiting and watching?* I pictured myself swooping down from above, picking off the enemy planes one by one. Then I imagined the thrill of landing, knowing I'd done my duty, that I'd played my part.

"Hey there, *le Raymond*!" The shout pulled me out of my daydream. It was my oldest brother, Bud, back from his Saturday job in the city. "And at which fine establishment will you be dining tonight, young sir?" he yelled.

Bud was always talking like that, adopting a bank manager's voice when he called me "young sir" and a French waiter's accent when he said *le Raymond*.

"Will you be joining us at home?"

"Maybe," I called as I slid from the thick branch. "But Goffie's cooking roast beef, so I don't know."

I edged along the limb as far as it would allow, just as I'd done a hundred times before, until the branches of one of the smaller trees were almost close enough to reach out and grab. Leaning forward, I let myself fall, pushing off from the beech with one hand while reaching out and grabbing onto the smaller tree with the other. It bent over gracefully, delivering me to the sidewalk in front of my sixteen-year-old brother.

To my satisfaction, Bud gave a little whistle of appreciation when I landed. "Not bad for an eight-year-old."

"Thanks," I replied. "Maybe I'll just come back with you and see what Mom's making."

Bud was twice my age and twice my height. I always had to skip along when I walked with him, frequently falling behind as he led the way past the timber houses with their wide verandas, filling up almost every inch of their narrow lots. At last we stepped off the street and onto the lane between two houses. To the left was 495 East Maynard Avenue, with the scent of slow-cooking beef coming out of Goffie's kitchen. To the right, in 493, there was the familiar smell of oatmeal hotcakes warming in the pan, almost ready to be drowned in honey. It was a difficult choice for a young boy to make.

Ever since I was small—too young to really remember— I had been able to eat from whichever kitchen I chose. It was an honor bestowed on only me. My three elder siblings weren't fed at Goffie's table—not even Bud. And as the years passed and three more Whipps children were added to the clan, none of them was given the open invitation either.

Goffie, a spinster of German origin who lived next door with her younger brother, had always had a sweet spot for me. She made me feel like her house was my second home. I had no way of knowing for sure, but perhaps the reason I was special to her was because she knew how lucky I was to be alive.

In the summer of 1924, as I was approaching my third birthday, I fell ill. My body ached and grew stiff, and a fever raged inside me. I lay sick for days, and nobody knew what was wrong with me or, even more important, how to help me recover. When the doctor finally diagnosed spinal meningitis, the only thing my parents and my worried neighbors could do was to make me comfortable and pray.

I don't have any memories of this time, but I was later told that when the fever was at its worst, I grew delirious. I began calling out, my voice filling every room of the house. I'd been ill for weeks, yet there was no mistaking what I was saying as I lay confined to my parents' bed: "I see Jesus."

Over and over I repeated the phrase. As I did so, the intensity of my parents' prayers increased. Finally, several weeks after I fell ill, I made a full recovery. God had saved me, plain and simple.

In time, Goffie's generosity extended beyond the occasional free meal. I was seven by the time my youngest sister, Jeanie, was born, and the struggle to fit the whole Whipps family in 493 East Maynard Avenue became virtually impossible. My eldest sister, Rite, had a tiny room of her own, and the next two boys, Bud and Glenn, took the second bedroom. That left just one room for me; my younger brother, Carl; my younger sister, Lois; and baby Jeanie—as well as my parents. It was Goffie who came up with the solution.

"Why doesn't Ray come and sleep over at my house," she said to my mom and dad. "He can have his own room, and we'll feed him as well, if that helps."

Everyone agreed that it was the perfect solution, and that was that. Overnight I became a dual-home boy, blessed with a large and loving family, a room of my own, and the freedom to choose between what was being served by the two best cooks in the neighborhood. The only problem with the whole arrangement came on days when both oatmeal hotcakes and roast beef with mashed potatoes were served. Faced with such an impossible decision, I was left with only one option: I'd have to eat both.

There was another advantage to moving next door to Goffie's. As 1929 came to a close, the Great Depression began to squeeze our family's finances. My dad, Carl, worked hard to provide for us, but it was difficult to raise a family on a machinist's wage. The fact that Goffie didn't charge my parents a cent made a small difference to the family budget, and in those days, small differences could have a big impact.

Having dual residences meant that I was expected to do chores at home as well as chores next door. At Goffie's it was my job to gather the eggs laid by her Rhode Island Reds, being careful not to get pecked. I was pretty good at it, and my ability to dodge the angry beaks led to my family's nickname for me: Speedy.

That was about all I liked of poultry care. I felt nauseous whenever Goffie or her brother Dutch took one of the birds down to the basement, chopped off its head, and dipped the pulsing body in hot water before pulling out the feathers. I tried to shield my eyes as much as possible, and when it was time to undertake the mighty task of cleaning up after the killing, I still felt the urge to run outside for air. But I have to admit: when I sat down at the table to eat the bird, it was all worthwhile.

Apart from eating, sleeping, doing chores, and going to school, my life was centered on my family. Most Sundays we took the streetcar to the Baptist church downtown, where Dad was an elder. The only exception was when we were visiting with relatives in the Ohio farmland. On those Sundays we would visit my grandfather's small country church, crammed into the pews beside my cousins, uncles, aunts, and grandmother as my grandfather preached.

We weren't rich, but we had enough to get by. Goffie's generosity helped, as did the little plot of land we all worked to grow vegetables. I soon picked up both a paper route and a magazine route, and I started mowing lawns in the summer. I was busy, the way a young boy should be.

Though we were cushioned from the worst of the Great Depression, we weren't blind to it. The two railway lines that ran parallel to each other through town carried two very different types of passengers. One track hurried the wealthy all the way to New York, while the other limped along, hauling freight to and from Pennsylvania. As the boxcars rolled by, slowing down for their approach to the Columbus station, the stowaway passengers were in plain sight— sometimes inside the cars, other times on top of the train.

After I said good-bye to Bud and followed the smell of roasting beef into Goffie's house, I went upstairs and peered out my bedroom window into the backyard. What I saw made me stop: there were unfamiliar people on the Whipps property. Tumbling downstairs and leaping across the yard, I found my second-oldest brother, Glenn, in the kitchen, staring outside.

"What's going on?" I asked.

Now that I was closer, I could see that the three strangers weren't entirely unfamiliar. I'd seen others who looked like them riding in the boxcars. Maybe they weren't the exact same ones, but they were hoboes, all right. Their clothes were all ragged, and their faces—though clean shaven—were lined and tired.

"I don't know," Glenn said. "They just showed up and asked Mom if she could feed them."

I watched as my mother moved among them. First she handed out plates and spoons, then she gave them stew from the heavy black pot that was always on the stove. The guests ate in silence. Once they finished, I heard them offer their thanks and leave. That was it.

In the months that followed, these meals became a familiar ritual. Every couple of weeks there would be a thin-looking stranger or two at the back door, asking for food. Mom gave them whatever she had, while we kids stood and watched. And though we never knew what prompted those first visitors to knock on our door— or how others after them knew to stop—we became convinced that there was some secret hobo sign along the railway track telling the weary travelers that a free meal was available up ahead. Whatever it was that brought them to our home, Mom always made them feel welcome. She never said no.

It wasn't just hoboes who edged into my world through the cracks of a failing economy. Mom was a teacher before we kids were born, and then she stayed home to take care of us. But when I was little she took on part-time work as a housekeeper for the head trainer at Ohio State University. His son and I became friends, and I was soon invited to join the coach's son in watching football games from the bench. Even though I was far too light to be a football player myself, watching the games unfold just yards from my eyes ignited something within me. I could see the way some of the smallest men on the field were able to dart and dive, avoiding the giants who thundered toward them. So from then on, whether I was playing football, basketball, or baseball with the boys in the neighborhood, I concentrated on moving deftly to avoid the tackle, hustling into perfect scoring positions, and scrambling to the base. I willed myself to be light and fast, as if somehow I could escape the basic rules of the universe.

In some ways, I guess I was right. Not only had I pulled through my bout of spinal meningitis when the odds were against me, but I also managed to escape another potential brush with death a few years later when I was thirteen.

I had taken on a little extra work helping Goffie's youngest brother, Howard, with his milk deliveries on the weekends. Howard had started out with a horse and cart, but by the time I was ready to join him for a few cents a day, the horse had been replaced by a truck. Life was starting to move a little faster, and Howard always said that my quick feet and steady hands were a big help.

Rain or shine, snow or gale, Howard made his deliveries. Whenever there was no school, I went along to help him. At first it wasn't easy balancing on the running board on the passenger side, but I soon got the hang of it, jumping down before the truck stopped and then skipping off to deliver the milk. Howard barely had to idle the engine before I stepped back on and he drove to the next house.

One Saturday I was too sick to join Howard on his route. That was the day something went wrong.

I remember Goffie's face as she walked into my room later that morning. I was half asleep as she entered, but by the time she reached my bed, I could see that she was upset. Her face was tight and pale, her steps heavy. I sat up straight, waiting for the news.

"Howard's in the hospital. He had an accident," she said. "He had to swerve to avoid another vehicle and lost control of the truck. It rolled and ended up on the other side of the road."

I was silent, though I was a whirlwind of thoughts and emotions. I knew that if I hadn't been ill, I would have been on that truck too. Would I have stood a chance on that running board when the truck rolled over? I couldn't imagine a version of this scenario where I would make it out alive.

I silently thanked God for keeping me home that day and saving my life. But almost immediately this thought came into my mind: *What if I had been there to warn Howard? Could I have stopped him from rolling the truck?*

This brought me to the one question I could speak out loud. "Is he going to be okay?"

"We don't know." Goffie stood to leave the room. I knew she loved her brother, but she wasn't one to sugarcoat the truth.

It turned out that the injuries were severe but not life threatening. Howard stayed in the Ohio State hospital for months, but the doctors said there was nothing serious enough to prevent a full recovery.

I was profoundly affected by the accident, and every day I made the thirty-minute journey on foot from East Maynard Avenue to the hospital. Each time, I found Howard smiling at me as I approached his bedside.

"You know you don't have to visit me *every* day, Smiley," he told me on more than one occasion.

"I know," I said. "But it's the least I can do. Besides, I want to make sure you get better soon and start working. It's not good for a boy like me to see his income fall like this!"

Most of my memories from my childhood were much less dramatic, however. I was just an ordinary kid growing up in an ordinary neighborhood, and my days were filled with the simple pleasures of being a kid. But as I look back now, I can trace some themes that ran throughout my childhood—themes that would collide and connect in years to come.

As bare-kneed elementary school kids, my friends and I formed our very own marching band. I was often out front, assuming the lead as drum major while the rest of the crew marched behind, clanging wooden spoons on dented cooking pans. The adults leaned out the windows to clap and cheer, but I wasn't paying attention to our audience. I was focused on the important task of leadership.

A number of the members of the East Maynard Marching Band, as we called ourselves, were also members of the Knothole Gang. A group of ten of us guys would meet by the baseball stadium that was home to the Columbus Red Birds. We'd peer through the holes in the wooden fence so we could catch telescopic views of some of the legends of the game: Babe Ruth, Lou Gehrig, and others. At times we were allowed inside the gates free of charge, but even without our faces pressed against a rough-hewn pine fence, we were still the Knothole Gang. Back then, a gang wasn't a group of troublemakers, and it was nothing to be afraid of. A gang was like a family, and family always stuck together.

Every year the Ohio State Fair brought a touch of the exotic to Columbus. Lions with their tamers, elephants, trapeze artists, and clowns would parade through the city, drawing people to the circus tent. The crowds would exit wide eyed and open mouthed, already anticipating the circus's return the next summer.

But the circus didn't impress me all that much. The animals were interesting and I appreciated the athleticism of the acrobats, but even when I was young, there was one sight that would steal my breath like no other. While most of my friends were captivated by the circus, in my eyes, nothing could compare to the marvel of flight.

I'm sure my fascination with the sky was partially credited to a town that lay about a hundred miles to the northeast of Columbus. For it was up in Akron that America's battle plan to dominate the skies was being put into action.

The period between World War I and World War II was the golden age of airships, and when I was a child, these helium-filled whales of the sky were largely considered to be the future of air travel. And when the giant hangars at the Goodyear Airdock outside Akron produced the USS *Akron*, then the USS *Macon*, the world marveled. Human beings had never made something that could fly that was so large. But that wasn't all: these airships were loaded with machine guns and four or five Sparrowhawk biplanes. What better fuel could there be to fire a young boy's imagination?

Yet while these behemoths grabbed my attention, they didn't win my heart. I had no desire to climb into an airship and be so vulnerable to the elements or the enemy's bullets. No, I wanted to be a biplane pilot, a flying ace who could thread his French-made SPAD fighter plane through the clouds to dismantle the opposition. On land

I was lithe, agile, and able to twist away from any hands that would try to grab me as I played football on the street. Why wouldn't I want to move the same way in the sky?

It was my Uncle Daniels who undoubtedly—though perhaps unwittingly—played the biggest part in fueling my imagination. After he returned from the Great War—what many believed was the "war to end all wars"—my siblings and I peppered him with endless questions.

"Tell us about the war again, Uncle Daniels," we'd beg.

"Yeah! Like the time you found Germans in a trench . . ."

"And about how you'd take them prisoner . . ."

"Or how you'd shoot them!"

And so, without complaint, Uncle Daniels would drag his mind back to the muddy fields of the European countryside. He'd clamber back into the earth, into the filth and death of the trenches, and again face the horror of stepping out into no-man's-land. Sifting through his memories, he'd limp back to those times he'd stood face-to-face with an enemy soldier. None of it was appropriate or even possible for children to understand, but he humored us. Perhaps turning these traumas into children's stories and comic book adventures lessened the pain a little somehow.

I didn't grasp the magnitude of what he had experienced, but there was still a lot I was soaking in. I liked looking at the scuffed helmet my uncle kept hidden in a box, and whenever he pulled it out, I pictured the Germans with their hands in the air, meekly obeying the orders to stand down and fall in line.

But I also had a sense that war wasn't quite like it was in the games I played with my buddies. There was something about the way Uncle Daniels looked just before he'd stop answering questions. I may have been young, but I could tell that there was a terrifying side to war. It wasn't a game; it was dangerous and real.

I couldn't imagine ever having the courage to face war myself, but I figured I'd never have to. After all, we'd won the war to end all wars, right?

2

WHERE'S PEARL HARBOR?

I SAT IN THE PASSENGER SEAT as my buddy and I followed the Olentangy River upstream. It was a December morning in 1941, and the car offered little protection from the cold. It had been twenty-one degrees the night before, and even though the sky was cloudless and the sun was clear and bright, our feet felt icy against the floorboards. Still, I was as happy as I'd ever been. What was a little cold to a twenty-year-old out for a drive in his best friend's new car?

Behind the wheel of the '40 Chevy was my friend Forrest Day. He loved telling me about the grip of the whitewall tires, the length of the hood, and the quality of the engine that lay beneath it—except that his words

were occasionally drowned out by a loud grinding noise
as he struggled with the stick shift, which protruded from
the floor like a bent broom handle. Behind us, sitting in
the tan seats, were my sisters Lois and Jeanie. The girls were
chattering away in the back—about what, I didn't know.
But it was good to be spending some time with them
and the rest of my family. I'd been away too much lately.
I needed this.

I pulled my coat tighter around me and looked out the
window. We were heading up to Antrim Lake, and it hadn't
taken long to leave the city behind. The road was now
flanked by tall trees that stood guard by the river. Stripped
of their leaves, stark against an endless sky, they looked
even taller. If it had been summer, we'd have been going to
the lake to swim, but since it was cold, we just planned to
meet up with some other friends and shoot the breeze—
and give Forrest a chance to perfect his gear changes.

It had been a year or two since I'd left high school, and
I'd done some maturing in that time. I'd found a job with
Western Electric, and I'd grown accustomed to the rhythms
of my new life. I traveled to different towns in Ohio, going
from office to office and installing whatever telephone
equipment my supervisor told me to.

On top of the new job, I'd also found a new place
to live. I'd left East Maynard Avenue and found a room
downtown, and both the job and the relocation had come
at just the right time. During my years in high school and
just after graduation, I had made some choices I knew my

parents wouldn't approve of, and I sensed I was in danger of drifting. Not that I was doing anything too terrible—just pushing the boundaries.

One of my first rebellions was smoking. I was sixteen and trying to look like a man, and my brother Glenn caught me. It wasn't even a real cigar; it was something everyone called an Indian stogie—a catkin that grew on some of the local trees. I'd been trying to keep one lit one afternoon when Glenn, who had just returned from college, found me hiding out near the big beech tree at the end of the street.

"I'm taking you home to Dad." Without another word, he grabbed me by the shirt and marched me home.

We both knew there was no way Dad would keep his cool, and as expected, the belt came out. I was left nursing tender skin and vowing to give up the stogies for good—or at least until I had my own place and could smoke in private. Once I had a job and a room, I got a pipe. I also quit reading my Bible and attending church.

The smoking was never a serious thing; it was more of an outward sign of an inward struggle, and I never liked that I'd given in to a vice I'd always considered to be wrong—sinful, even. I also knew how disappointed my folks would be if they found out. It was just that my life was no longer making sense. For the first time in my life, God seemed far away. The Bible wasn't speaking to me the way it once had, and prayers felt awkward on my lips. Piece by piece, I watched my faith begin to weaken.

When I was a child, life had felt so safe as I jumped back and forth between Goffie's house and my own. I remembered how certain I'd felt in my faith back then—how I'd vowed to follow God, resist temptation, and keep myself pure. Now life seemed a lot more complicated.

What had changed? It wasn't that God no longer seemed real; it was that I doubted whether the Lord was up to the job at hand. I wasn't alone, either. For many of my peers, history was conspiring to make life even more turbulent. War—even if it was halfway across the world—was making everybody nervous.

When I was in high school, news about the situation in Europe started taking center stage. Week after week, as conditions intensified overseas, I joined in the lunchtime conversations with my friends.

"How could those countries get taken over so fast?" I would ask of no one in particular.

My friends had their own questions.

"Why don't they just fight back instead of letting themselves get taken over?"

"If Hitler was trying to invade America, he wouldn't last five minutes."

But beneath the teenage bravado and cheap talk, we all knew the war was no joke. There was good reason to fear Hitler and Mussolini, and even if we didn't voice our fears, we suspected that at some point America would get pulled in.

And so, as the war progressed, our conversations became

more specific, turning to what each of us would do to fight back against the German army.

"US Army, all the way. Gimme a gun, and I'd mow them down in a heartbeat."

"Nah. I'd sign up for the Navy. I'd take out those U-boats and leave them to drown."

But neither of these got my vote. "I wouldn't be anything other than a pilot," I insisted. "You'd never catch me on the ground or trapped in a boat. Never."

Back in Forrest's Chevy, I thought about how much had changed since those conversations in the school cafeteria. The war in Europe had escalated, and I'd already seen families say goodbye to their sons who had chosen to go over and fight. Something had changed in me as I'd watched them go. In some ways this sobering turn of events had woken me from my stupor. Based on the way the war was going, I figured I would have to enlist or get drafted at some point, and I didn't want to go through something like that without my faith fully intact. Lately I'd stopped smoking and visiting bars. I'd also started going back to church, and I was reading my Bible again. It felt good to have my life back on track.

America was still technically enjoying peacetime, but that peace felt tenuous at best. It was no secret that each branch of the military was significantly increasing its troops and equipment. During this time of general unease, I found that my Bible was once more a source of real help. I'd turn to the thirty-seventh psalm and draw comfort from the declaration that the wicked and unrighteous would face their just judgment. This psalm also spoke to me of God's faithfulness more meaningfully than ever: "The salvation of the righteous is of the LORD; he is their strength in the time of trouble" (verse 39). The words were like sunlight to my soul.

As the war escalated, the story of Joshua took on new meaning for me. The Old Testament describes him as a warrior—both a great commander and a loyal follower. I appreciated that Joshua was both tactically astute and humbly dependent on God. If there was a model for getting through war with body and soul intact, surely it was Joshua.

By Christmas 1941, war had edged its way into the Whipps family. Over the previous year, Mom had been working temporarily for the registration board, helping with the mammoth task of issuing the draft. She had signed up both Bud and Glenn as soon as they were eligible, and each time, the newspaper had sent a photographer to capture the moment. The press loved these patriotic stories.

Signing up for the draft didn't necessarily mean that a young man would get picked, but there was no surprise when, not long after their visit to the draft board, the postman delivered brown envelopes addressed first to Bud and then later to Glenn. We called these letters "greetings," although thinking about it now, it seems like a more optimistic name than they deserved. Perhaps it was an attempt to soften the truth that the recipient was being sent to war.

Whatever personal feelings the letters stirred, public support for the war was high. We all knew that the German-Italian alliance was a threat to the United States, and with France having already fallen to Germany, it was clear that the Allies had quite a fight on their hands. Signing up to do one's duty, whether that meant fighting, taking a job in a factory, or serving in some other way, was an act of patriotism.

As soon as Forrest pulled into the parking lot at the lake, I knew something was wrong. Typically people parked and then headed down to the water, but that day everyone was huddled together around the cars, talking over one another or leaning in to listen to radios.

"What's going on?" Forrest said as he pulled up alongside a Ford sedan. "Why isn't anyone down at the lake?"

"You didn't hear?" A girl who looked to be about my age scrunched up her face in disbelief. "Pearl Harbor has been attacked."

Forrest pulled his head back into the car and repeated the news for the benefit of the girls in the back. Silence fell for a second, and then Jeanie spoke up.

"What's Pearl Harbor?"

More silence.

"I don't know," I said, looking at an equally confused Forrest. "But it doesn't sound good."

It didn't take long to find out, and before the end of the following day, the significance of the attack was clear to all of us. President Roosevelt's voice boomed through the radio. There would be no more delay, no more doubt. America was at war.

We weren't the only family in America who felt weighed down by a strange heaviness as Christmas 1941 approached. It was as if all the trees and the presents and the food were somehow irrelevant—as if we were playing a game when there was far more important work to be done.

All seven of us children were at home on Christmas Eve, and it felt good to be under one roof again, taken care of by Mom and Dad. For those of us old enough to understand what was going on, there was one unanswerable question hanging in the air: Would this be the last time such a gathering would be possible?

We sat in silence that evening, listening to the radio as it relayed a special broadcast that featured Girl Scouts, Boy Scouts, and eventually Winston Churchill. But what I remember most was when President Roosevelt leaned in toward the microphone and addressed the nation. His speech perfectly articulated the trauma, confusion, and anger felt by so many of us. Yet somehow he managed to move from empathy to exhortation, urging people to prepare for the year to come by preparing their hearts:

> Therefore, I . . . do hereby appoint the first day of the year 1942 as a day of prayer, of asking forgiveness for our shortcomings of the past, of consecration to

the tasks of the present, of asking God's help in days
to come. We need His guidance that this people may
be humble in spirit but strong in the conviction of
the right; steadfast to endure sacrifice, and brave to
achieve a victory of liberty and peace.

When the draft had first been approved in September
1940—the first in peacetime during the history of the
United States—the age range was set between twenty-one
and forty-five. Bud and Glenn had both been old enough,
but I was only nineteen. However, in the days following the
attack on Pearl Harbor, legislation was passed to expand
the selective service system to cover all men between the
ages of eighteen and sixty-four. Overnight I became eligible
to fight.

A few days after Christmas, on a Sunday afternoon, I
picked up Mom and made the journey to the draft office
that had been set up in a museum on the Ohio State
campus. Having worked at Western Electric for the better
part of a year, I'd finally been able to save enough money to
buy my own car. I'd ended up with a Chevy sedan, similar
to Forrest's but a little older. I was intent on keeping it pris-
tine and shining like a black beetle, and it felt good to be
able to take Mom out like this, especially since my parents
had never had a car of their own.

I was just as well groomed as my car, wearing a dark,
double-breasted suit and tie, and having taken extra care to
slick my hair back to complete the Bing Crosby and Sam

Edwards look. Once again, the reporter was there, asking questions and taking a photo.

"Just be natural," he said. "Pretend like you're signing the bottom of the forms, okay?"

Mom projected nothing but patriotism and pride, even managing to work up a smile for the camera, but I found it harder to hide my true feelings.

Suddenly I didn't feel quite as confident as my clothes suggested. My hands froze over the paper, my eyes looking directly at the camera. Was I ready for such a commitment? I really wasn't sure.

Fort George Wright
Spokane, Washington

November 10, 1943

Dear Mom and Dad,

Well, I made it! I'm here in Fort George Wright, and I couldn't be happier. Everything's going well so far. It's wet, but that's one thing about us Portland folks—we're not afraid of a little rain, are we?

What I'm not so used to is being in the Army. We're in the middle of basic training right now, and all of it has been new for me. We've had two weeks of drills and classes, learning everything from military courtesy to how to put on a gas mask. We've hardly been near a patient, but after tomorrow we'll start working at the wards for two weeks. After that, if all goes well, we graduate.

Every day starts with an hour of calisthenics, then we march and drill and make our way around in formation just like regular soldiers. At first I found it hard not to laugh, but I knew I'd get in real trouble if I did. When they gave us fatigues to replace our traditional nurse's uniform, it helped a bit. It's a little easier to take things seriously when you're dressed like a soldier.

I'm surrounded by girls who are just like me. We've all finished our nurse's training, and we're eager to get out and serve. All of us want in so badly.

I know that going to war is not something to be taken lightly, but even after being here just a few days, I know this is the right place for me. Before I found out I was being sent here, I was so frustrated that I had to stay home and that I couldn't do anything to help when our boys were fighting. And when Chuck got in the Navy, it made me so cross. To have my little brother accepted when the Navy had turned me down seemed unfair. I wanted to be like Chuck and cousin Rog and Stan. I wanted to do my bit—I still do.

I've been thinking about why I've been so desperate to sign up. I guess it's partly because everyone else is pitching in to do their part, but there's more to it than that. Ever since war broke out, I've been thinking a lot about Aunt Jo, remembering when she'd come back from Argentina full of stories about her life there. For so long I wanted to be a missionary just like her. I didn't tell you this part, but I was sure I wanted to go to Alaska or Africa or somewhere else far away and do something that would help people. And I believed that was something God wanted me to do too.

I've also learned a lot from both of you about doing hard things when necessary. I know it wasn't easy when I was growing up and money was tight. Remember how I had one dress and one pair of shoes, and how in winter whenever my feet got wet you'd add another strip of cardboard into them? You didn't complain about being poor; you just did what you had to do. I think I've learned some of that from you. I feel like there's a need in the world that I can do my part to help with. It doesn't feel like a sacrifice, and it doesn't feel like a risk. It's just something I have to do.

I think that's why I was so mad when the Navy turned me down. I felt as though this dream I'd had was being thrown in the trash. I should have trusted God though. He had a plan for me, and I know He's placed me in the Army for a reason.

Today during breakfast we were talking about which theater we'll end up serving in. We all want to go to Europe, and I'm sure that's because the news of what the boys have experienced over there has touched us all. But when it comes down to it, I just want to go where God wants me.

I'm going to end now. We have to get our drills perfect tomorrow, and I need to be alert or I might turn right when I mean to turn left!

Say hi to the boys and give them a hug from me. I know you'll remember me in your prayers, just as I remember you in mine.

Love,
Betty

3

"DON'T SHOW ME UP, YOU LITTLE TWERP!"

EVEN THOUGH I'D ENLISTED for the Navy Air Corps, I had to wait until there was room for me to begin the cadet training program. So that's what I did. I watched as 1942 edged by, one month at a time, and as I continued my normal routine of working at Western Electric, my fear of war started to fade. In its place, my mind was flooded with thoughts of what it would be like to become an actual fighter pilot. I had never once taken a commercial flight, let alone piloted an aircraft, so there was a lot to be excited about.

It took almost a whole year before I was finally called to Ohio Wesleyan, thirty minutes north of Columbus.

Wearing the officer's uniform I'd been given—although one with a star on the sleeve instead of stripes—I joined the fifty other cadets in the mess hall as we listened to the briefing. A fit-looking man in his forties was at the front, explaining the aviation cadet course and what we'd be expected to do.

"Landing a fighter plane on a moving aircraft carrier is one of the most difficult technical tasks anyone in the forces will be expected to accomplish. Cadets, this is the V-5 program, and you're at the start of a long and difficult twelve months. You will be tested and observed throughout, and you're going to need to study like you've never studied before."

The longer the officer spoke, the smaller the room felt. Months of fantasizing about being a pilot evaporated in seconds.

"You're here for the next three months. We'll teach you the theory of flying, but not much else. After that, assuming you can keep up, you'll be moved to two more locations for proper flight training. Pass those, and you'll be tested at the new facility in Pensacola, Florida. At the end of all that, if you're good enough at flying and you have an A average in math, we'll give you your wings."

The officer kept talking, and I heard him say something about weekend passes, but I didn't take in anything else. My mind was still stuck on the image of trying to land a plane on an aircraft carrier as it rose and fell on the ocean swell. I'd never thought about that before. In all my imaginings of myself as a pilot, I envisioned myself sitting eagle-like above the battle, swooping down to pick off the enemy before rising into the safety of the clouds. I hadn't considered that I'd have to get the thing out of the sky, let alone make it land on a target as precise as a moving aircraft carrier.

As the briefing wrapped up, the officer invited us to ask questions. This was all so different from what I'd expected. I thought that there would be red-faced drill sergeants forcing us to crawl through the mud, but if this meeting was any indication, that wouldn't be the tone here. We weren't being treated as equals to the officers, but we weren't being shouted at like lowlifes either.

My first impressions turned out to be correct. Throughout my time in the V-5 program, we were made to work hard but we were treated much better than the Army infantrymen, who were also being trained at Ohio Wesleyan. We were given better rations, and we ate the same meat and fish with fresh vegetables that the officers ate. The enlisted infantrymen got beans and not much more. And while they were crammed together in large dormitories, we were housed in smaller rooms, with only four or five men to a room. To my surprise, the infantrymen even saluted us V-5 cadets. I'd never gone to college, so I couldn't say how life as a cadet compared, but between the rigorous study and the atmosphere of camaraderie, I felt sure this must be a pretty close match.

Best of all, though, were the planes. Even though we had no time in the air at Ohio Wesleyan, just looking at the aluminum Luscombes on the ground was enough to fill me with a sense of freedom and excitement. I was sure flying would come easily, and I had no doubt my academics would fall into place too. As the first three months drew to a close, I allowed myself to dream a little more seriously about getting my wings.

When nobody was dropped at the end of the first part of the course, I felt even more confident about the next phase. When it was time to move on, the cadets were scattered to a number of different locations across the country. I was sent to Washington State, where the Navy Air Corps had taken over Gonzaga University, an old Jesuit school in Spokane. I was excited to be heading to the West Coast—farther from home than I'd ever been before. This adventure had even more appeal for me because everyone knew Bing Crosby had a house that backed up to the grounds there.

So far, my naval training was everything I'd hoped it would be. My new instructors told me I was doing well, and after a total of just eight hours of flying with an instructor by my side, I was allowed to fly solo—the first one in my group. Climbing into the two-seater Luscombe, with an empty seat to my right where there had previously always been an officer, I felt like I didn't even need wings to fly this machine.

As I taxied to the end of the runway and prepared for takeoff, my nerves kicked in. But it wasn't long before they were left behind, along with the ground. Alone in the cockpit, alone in the sky, I was free. If it weren't for the limited fuel, I could have spent all day up there.

Back on land, there were congratulations to receive from the officers and the ritual dunking in an old bathtub that had been abandoned outside by some previous cadets.

"Every time someone makes their first flight alone, they get thrown into a tub full of ice-cold water," an officer explained as everyone gathered round. "But only those who have already soloed get to throw him. Whipps, you're up."

With that, a handful of officers reached out and grabbed me, easily lifting this newbie pilot over to the bathtub. It was cold all right, but no amount of shivering could have wiped the smile from my face.

Flying wasn't the only thing that was going well for me at Gonzaga. The demands of the physical training had increased, and I was thriving. The obstacle course was rumored to be the toughest in the whole Navy Air Corps, yet somehow I was able to scramble up the walls, sprint across the trails, and climb the ropes faster than most of the other guys. When a local newspaper came to take photos of the V-5 program in action, the officers gave me the nod to demonstrate for the camera. Whether I was hanging from ropes as thick as my wrist or swinging across the monkey bars set three feet apart and ten feet off the ground, the physical maneuvers just came naturally to me. It wasn't flying, but it felt pretty close.

Once the action shots had been taken, the photographer had us change into our uniforms and line up on the steps at the front of the college.

"You sure this is going to be in the papers?" I whispered to a colleague as we shuffled into position.

"That's what the man said. Why?"

"I want my parents to know which one's me." I pulled off my peaked cap and tucked it under my belt in the back of my trousers. When the photo came out, I discovered I wasn't the only cadet with this plan. Three of us were without hats, eight were wearing the wrong color tie, and most of our uniforms were wrinkled and creased. On top of that, the majority of us were smiling and looking relaxed, making the V-5 program seem more like a collection of college grads at a theme party than a bunch of future fighter pilots.

If the atmosphere back at Ohio Wesleyan had been relaxed, then Gonzaga was even more so. The university was run by Jesuit priests, and along with permission to rent the buildings, the Navy Air Corps had also been given the services of Father Duseau, one of the priests. He led us in morning calisthenics, and I loved every minute of those sessions. Father Duseau often picked me to lead the men out as we went for a run. Whenever we approached the edge of Bing Crosby's property, we strained to catch a glimpse of him, but we never did.

And when Father Duseau, whose second-floor room was just above the cadets' quarters, was frequently awakened by the sound of my clambering in through the window at night, having returned from a not-quite-legal trip into town, the priest would only ever greet me the next day with a smile and the words, "Did you have a good time in town last night, Whipps?" I never drank or smoked on any of these trips; the camaraderie with the other guys was enough of a lure.

When it came to flying, however, things were serious. We knew that landing on an aircraft carrier would require a high level of skill and would offer zero margin of error—we'd heard that so many times over the past several months that we could recite it in our sleep. But once we were at Gonzaga, we found out precisely how hard it was. The technique required the pilot to be able to approach at the perfect speed, stall the engine at the perfect time, and touch down at the perfect spot to allow the plane's landing gear to catch on the cable strung across the deck. Once hooked onto the cable, the plane would be brought to a sudden stop a short way down the five-hundred-foot landing strip. If you hit the cable too fast or missed it entirely, and if you couldn't get up enough speed to take off again by the time you ran out of strip, there was virtually nothing to prevent you and your plane from going into the ocean. With the carrier traveling at speeds of up to eighteen knots (twenty miles per hour), there was almost no way you'd make it out alive.

The Navy Air Corps wanted its pilots to be skilled and bold and undeterred by fear, so as soon as we'd mastered the basics of flight, we were encouraged to experiment.

Our instructors would send us out in our planes alone—
with no instructor, no partner, and no radio. We had just
a parachute and a whole lot of trust. And while sometimes
the instructors would be flying nearby, they often just told
us to head out five or ten miles and get to work. We had
to learn how to put the plane into a spin and, more important, how to get out of it at just the right time. There were
loops to master and turns to perfect—the tools we would
rely on in combat. We had to learn how to control the
plane the way we would control a fishing rod: by placing it
exactly where we wanted it every time.

Being able to stall the plane successfully was essential.
By turning on the carburetor heat, we could keep the
engine running while at the same time stopping the propellers to reduce speed. That meant we could put the plane
into a spin to avoid enemy fire. It also meant that when we
were trying to land, if we didn't manage to hook the plane
onto the cable that ran across the flight deck, we could kick
the propellers back to life and fly off again before making
another attempt.

One day when I was alone in the skies above Washington
State, I was practicing going from a stall into a spin. It was
a move I'd carried out many times before, and since it was
a clear day with good weather, I really had no excuse for
doing something as foolish as forgetting to turn on the
carburetor heat before disengaging the propellers. Yet that's
exactly what I did. Within seconds the engine stopped,
leaving a strange silence that iced through the cockpit.

Momentarily frozen, my body screaming with adrenaline, I realized what I had done. I was three thousand feet above the ground in an aluminum can without any power. Everything was silent for a few seconds as the plane gave in to the strong arms of gravity that were hauling it back down to earth.

The nose of my plane was pointing straight up, leaving me staring at the faint traces of clouds high above. As the plane plummeted, a new noise began to fill the void left by the dying engine. It was the sound of wind. While the plane was sucked down toward the earth, the whooshing noise grew louder and louder. I seriously doubted I was going to make it.

We had been taught in flight training that if ever we got into trouble in the air, we should try to find a spot to land. Straining my neck in both directions, I looked for somewhere flat enough and clear enough, but all I could see were five-thousand-foot mountains that were covered in trees. Twisting in my seat, I finally caught the faintest glimpse of a field. It was my only chance.

Somehow, I wasn't too worried about dying. If I crashed, I knew I'd go to heaven, which didn't seem too bad. What made every muscle in my body clench was the thought of what would happen if I made it out alive. If I crashed the plane, I'd wash out of the program, and I really didn't want that to happen.

As I tried to bring the plane under control, it occurred to me that there was one more thing I could try. I'm still not sure whether it was something I'd heard in a lecture or something I'd been told by an instructor on one of my accompanied flights, but I figured I had nothing to lose. I threw the switch that turned the carburetor heat back on, swallowed hard, and pushed the joystick forward, sending the plane into a dive. Everything about the move went against my instinct for self-preservation, but it was my only hope.

I stared at the propeller in front of the cockpit and tried to ignore the sight of the ground just beyond it. Then, almost magically, the propeller started to turn again. My ears filled with the sound of the engine charging back to life, and the tension that had gripped my stomach vanished in an instant.

When I was sure I'd regained control, I pulled out of the dive and made the ten miles back to base. I landed carefully and taxied to the hangar. There was no need to tell any of the instructors, and as soon as I could, I lay down on my cot and thanked God for keeping me safe. You only make a mistake like that once. Even more than the formal lessons I'd learned about stalls and spins and how to keep an engine running, that was the day I learned not to let my mind wander. If I was going to survive the war, I would have to learn how to pour all my concentration into the moment in front of me.

The three months at Gonzaga passed quickly, and while I was disappointed that a few of my fellow cadets were dropped from the V-5 program, I was grateful to have passed. Now it was on to the third location for training, where we would perfect our flying and come to grips with the complex math required of pilots. This time I was sent south to Saint Mary's College near Berkeley, California. For a boy from Columbus, the idea of being stationed in the beautiful hills near San Francisco sounded almost too good to be true—especially when I was told that the debutantes from Berkeley were going to join us for a dance one evening soon after we arrived.

Tradition stated that one cadet from each class would lead the dancing, and somehow the honor that year was mine. Even though I was in the best shape of my life, this was one physical challenge I felt wholly unequipped to deal with. I'd never been much of a dancer, and the thought of being in the spotlight made me profoundly nervous. Still, I did as I was told and filled in my name, height, and weight on the card I was given. Apparently these cards would ensure that dancers were paired up correctly.

What I didn't realize until I stepped out onto the dance floor was that one of my colleagues had seen this as a prime opportunity to play a trick on me, and he'd made some significant edits to my vital statistics. So while my dance partner was expecting a six-foot-two, 200-pound specimen of male perfection, instead she got a gangly guy of five foot ten and 140 pounds who barely filled out his uniform.

There was no hiding the disappointment in her eyes. "Why did you lie?" she whispered as we fumbled our way through a waltz to the sounds of barely suppressed laughter. All I could do was smile, shrug, and hope the moment would pass quickly.

When it came to flying, life at Saint Mary's was more competitive than it was at Gonzaga. Perhaps this was because the program was getting tougher, or perhaps it was simply due to the new mix of personnel, with personalities that often clashed. Either way, the officers had started reminding us how hard it was going to be to pass the course—as if we needed reminding.

As I heard more about the demanding study requirements, I was growing increasingly concerned. And for the first time, I also found myself unable to get along with a fellow cadet.

His name was Wetzler. Like me, he was from Ohio—only his part of town was far nicer than my neighborhood. Since our names were Wetzler and Whipps, we often found ourselves paired up for physical training. We had to pull each other out of the water for lifeguard drills, which was easy enough for Wetzler but a challenge for me, given that my partner had played high school football and was pushing 175 pounds. It was even harder when he wouldn't cooperate. He'd just hang in the water while I tried to haul him out, a wise-guy smirk painted all over his face.

Wetzler may have had it easier in the pool, but the advantage was mine when it came to putting on our tennis shoes, shorts, and T-shirts and heading out to run.

As we lined up one morning, we were given these

instructions: "Run a mile in six minutes, or you'll have to do it again."

Wetzler leaned toward me as we prepared to start. "Don't show me up and run fast, you little twerp."

I just shrugged and made my way to the front of the group, clocking the six minutes with a few seconds to spare. My partner was not so swift, however, and he didn't make the time limit.

Wetzler got his revenge on me a few days later when we were playing soccer. Going in too hard and too high for a block, he kicked my knees out from behind me and laid me flat out on the grass. I had to be helped off the field, and though my injury didn't hinder my progress in the program, it did put a temporary hold on my participation in sports.

Inside I was steamed for a few days, but I never bad-mouthed him. I'd been brought up better than that. And whether we liked it or not, we were both on the same team.

Flying had become a part of me by now. The hours I spent perfecting my maneuvers were the best way to escape the nagging feelings that caught up with me whenever I was on the ground. Up in the sky I felt peaceful and free, but as soon as I landed and entered the classroom, my worries came crashing down on top of me.

The academic demands of the program had increased significantly since I'd moved to California, and with the addition of trigonometry and calculus, I was struggling to keep up. Such a high standard for math was vital for a Navy Air Corps pilot, as there were numerous calculations to be made both when landing and when taking off. But even though I understood why it was essential to be able to work out the velocity required for takeoff given the weight of fuel the plane was carrying and the speed at which the aircraft carrier was traveling, it didn't make the classes any easier.

So I wasn't entirely surprised when one afternoon I was called to the commander's office. As I waited in the corridor outside, I was joined by nine other cadets—including Wetzler. Some, like me, were also having a hard time with the math, but others had no academic struggles at all. What reason could there be for all of us to meet with the commander like this? As I looked around, I realized that all these guys were from Ohio, but what could that have to do with anything?

Before any of us managed to figure it out, the door opened and all ten of us were called in.

The commander didn't waste time with pleasantries. "Now you all know that anybody who washes out of the program at any point ends up as a second-class seaman."

I felt my chest tighten. I knew this; everyone did. It was one of the awkward truths about the V-5 program: those who had hoped to conquer the skies as a Navy pilot but failed were immediately retrained and sent to war packed in one of the Navy's ships or—even worse—in one of their submarines. It's true that if we earned our wings, we would still be based on a ship, but life as an officer pilot on a huge aircraft carrier was worlds apart from that of a second-class seaman on a tiny frigate.

On top of that loss of prestige and responsibility, I had another reason for not wanting to be a seaman: I was prone to seasickness. I figured I'd make do on a big ship, but I couldn't imagine how green I'd be on a sub.

The commander went on. "Well, for you boys from Ohio, things have been somewhat different. I'm sure none of you read the small print when you signed up for the program, but if you had, you would know that you have an option at any point to request to be honorably discharged. Don't ask me why Ohio did things differently, but that's the way it is." He paused, looking around the room. "But now things are changing. You've got two more weeks to get the honorable discharge, but after that, you stay the course and take your chances like the rest of them."

This was all news to me, and it left me feeling both shocked and troubled. Two weeks felt like too short a time to decide whether I would give up on my lifelong dream of being a pilot. How could I be expected to make that kind of decision? But if I was honest with myself, I could see the warning signs when it came to my academic studies. Was I confident I could get an A average when I'd barely heard of trigonometry and calculus prior to arriving at Saint Mary's?

As we filed out, I wondered out loud, "I'm still struggling with all that higher math. Maybe this is where it all ends for me."

"Are you kidding me?" The words came from a young cadet I'd spoken to a few times. "This is great news. Remember Joey, who washed out midway through Gonzaga? He wrote me and said he was offered this option too. As soon as he got home, he went to an air base in Columbus and took the exam, and now he's flying with those guys." He thumped me on the back. "Think about it, Whipps. How much math do you need when you're taking off and landing in a field?"

It all sounded good, but the decision still weighed heavily on me. This was a tough choice for me to make on my own, even if I was already twenty-one. I wished I'd worked harder at math while I was in school, especially since my mom had been a teacher and would have helped me. Yet I'd never felt the urge to really push myself in school. I had no way of knowing back then that my future as a pilot could rest on trigonometry formulas.

I was torn. Did I need to apply myself to study and work harder than ever, hoping I'd make it to Florida and beyond? It was a risk, but weren't pilots supposed to take risks?

Then again, I had to admit that the alternative looked a lot better. A pilot was still a pilot, whether he took off from water or land. And if this route was a guarantee that I wouldn't end up trapped in an oversized tin can along with hundreds of other sailors, surely that was worth it, wasn't it?

Both arguments played out in my mind, but just when the balance seemed to shift one way, I would reconsider and find myself leaning toward the other option. The clock was ticking, and I was desperate for help. So I went to the one source of wisdom that had never let me down: I prayed to God.

The conviction came gradually, like the dawning of the first light, but I knew what I needed to do. It was time to head back to the draft office.

4

THE RELUCTANT DOGFACE

MY SECOND VISIT TO THE DRAFT BOARD could not have been more different from the first. Having sold my '38 Chevy before entering the V-5 program and turning down my mother's offer of company, I approached the squat building in a corner of the Ohio State campus alone and on foot. There were no photographers on hand to document the moment. Then again, there was also no pulsing knot of fear like the one I'd tried to suppress when I'd been here almost a year earlier. With seven months in the Navy Air Corps and sixty hours of flying time behind me, I felt confident.

As I was invited to sit down opposite a kind-looking lady a little younger than my mother, I caught myself revisiting some of those old dreams of flying high above the ground and picking off the enemy.

I told her about the Navy Air Corps and the honorable discharge, but before I could finish, she interrupted. "So now you want to enroll in the Army Air Corps?"

"Yes, ma'am," I replied. Was it good news that she had been able to guess what I was aiming for? Maybe that was a sign that I had a good chance of being accepted. As the woman made some notes on the form in front of her, I searched her face for a sign. Finding none, I looked around. Last time I'd been here, the room was quiet and somber, like a bank. Now it was more like a factory, bustling with dozens of people trying to process an increased workload. This war was serious business, and its appetite for personnel was insatiable.

"Well, you've just missed this month's entry exam." The woman put down her pencil and looked at me. "But you can wait and take it in a few weeks. I'll make sure you don't get drafted in the meantime."

My spirits were high as I told my parents about the plan, and in the days that followed, I could feel myself relax. Even though I missed flying and it felt odd to be back in civilian clothes, it was good to be home. In two or three months I'd be back in the air, preparing to serve my country. But in the meantime, I was a free man in Columbus.

Not much had changed in the eight months that I'd been away, as most of my friends hadn't enlisted. But there

were a couple of old friends I wanted to catch up with.
Dale Jensen, a buddy from high school, was one of them.
He'd become a B-17 pilot, and he must have been good,
since he'd been given the task of flying General Twining,
the US Air Force Chief of Staff, wherever he needed to go.
Dale was home on leave, and he and I met to talk about
flying and the war and everything else that mattered.
Even though I had no desire to lug one of those great big
bombers around the sky, I found it reassuring to talk to a
pilot who had been in combat and had come back alive
and well.

Less than two weeks after my solo visit to the draft
board, I came home to find my mother standing uncharac-
teristically still in the kitchen.

"This came for you," she said, handing me a brown
envelope.

It looked familiar, but not in a good way. I forced a
smile and mumbled my thanks. Joining my mother at the
table, I resisted the urge to rip open the envelope. I was
confused, and I felt the first whispers of panic starting to
rise within me. I tried to convince myself that it was just a
letter confirming my date for the Army Air Corps examina-
tion, or perhaps it was some paperwork having to do with
my discharge from the Navy. But it was too early for the
first and the wrong color envelope for the second. Still,
whatever it was, I knew that rushing wouldn't help. I'd
learned that at Gonzaga: stay calm, breathe, think.

The air inside me turned to lead the moment I read the

letter's heading. Spread across the page beneath the draft board seal were these words:

ORDER TO REPORT FOR INDUCTION

My name followed, and then the word that seemed so mightily out of place:

Greetings. . . . You have been selected for training and service in the Army.

How it had happened, I couldn't quite understand. But sure enough, I'd been drafted into the Army as an infantry-man before I'd even had a chance to take the Army Air Corps exam. The letter said I was to report to Fort Hayes for training in two weeks.

My mom picked up the letter and read it, her face still set in the same tense expression.

Stuffing the greetings into my pocket, I walked out of the house. Within a dozen feet I began running, headed to the university campus and the draft board. I didn't slow down for the whole two miles; I didn't need to, and I didn't want to. After all, I was in the best shape I'd ever been in. Fit enough to be a fighter pilot, that's for sure.

The office was still open when I arrived, although there was a long line ahead of me. I used the wait to calm down and scan the room for the woman I'd met with when I was here last. There was no sign of her. Finally I was invited to talk to an older man with a tired look in his eyes.

"I just got this," I explained, pushing the greetings toward the man. "But I'm waiting to take the exam for the Army Air Corps." I did my best to explain about my previous visit and the woman who told me she would make sure that *this*—I waved the letter—wouldn't happen. The man looked on, unimpressed. Eventually he agreed to check the file. I sat and waited, forcing my breathing to slow down. The place looked like it did a couple of weeks earlier: busy. Maybe even busier.

When the man returned some minutes later, I could tell by the look on his face that there was no reason to get my hopes up.

"She didn't make a note in your file," he said. "And she doesn't work here anymore. There's nothing we can do. You're in, soldier."

With that, the discussion was over.

The two weeks that separated the greetings from my departure felt crushing. In an instant, my dream of becoming a pilot was over. My flying experience would count for nothing as an enlisted man, and the closest I'd get to a plane was if I was jumping out of one. It was over, pure and simple.

This new path was certainly not one I would have chosen. The reports coming back from the Pacific painted a picture of relentless fighting against a merciless enemy in brutal conditions. What soldier would want to sign up for such a task? Even if I ended up on the ground as an infantryman in Europe, I wondered how I would cope.

I would never try to avoid my duty—far from it. In fact, I was proud to sign up and serve, and I saw it as my duty—as both an American and a Christian—to do so. But was I cut out for life as a soldier? Could I handle myself on the battlefield? It was one thing to shoot down a plane, but killing a man standing in front of you was something else entirely. Could I do it?

Days passed slowly, as did the nights, but there was one thing that took my mind off the Army. Having heard about my situation, Dale took me out one day, and the two of us ended up wandering around Lazarus, a department store downtown. I was looking at something I had no interest in buying when Dale dug into my side with his elbow.

"Ray, look at that girl over there—over behind the counter." I looked up and saw who Dale was pointing at. She was beautiful, that much was true.

"I know her," I said. "She used to be Forrest's girl. She goes to my church."

"Quit messing around, Ray."

But I wasn't messing around, and to prove it, I pulled Dale, who was dressed in his full uniform, over to the counter. I smiled at the girl.

"Colleen," I announced as she looked up, "meet my friend Captain Dale Jensen."

I stood back while Dale and Colleen spoke. It was only

a matter of minutes before Dale invited her to dinner and Colleen said yes. After the date, when I asked Dale how it had gone, I wasn't all that surprised when Dale told me that he was going to ask her to marry him.

If she said yes, he wanted to get married before he had to return to his duties with General Twining.

"It's war, Ray," he said. "And none of us have as much time as we used to."

Just as he said, Dale and Colleen set a wedding date just two weeks away. I had already reported for training at Fort Hayes in Columbus, but Dale, having asked me to be his best man, used his influence to get me off-site for the wedding.

It was a beautiful day—one of those November mornings that starts out cold but clear—and for the few hours we were together for the ceremony, I forgot all about the world of Fort Hayes and my life in the Army.

In no time, though, I had to go back and prepare to fight—no longer as a cadet, but as a soldier. After eight months of being trained in the art of flying solo, I was jolted by how different my new life was. Where the Navy Air Corps was intent on nurturing a sense of courage, skill, and independent thinking among its pilots, Army infantry training was designed to create units. Obeying orders was vital, even if those orders failed to make sense. Individualism played second fiddle to requirements.

After a week or two at Fort Hayes, I was sent south to the sprawling campus of Camp Blanding, Florida. I tried not to think about the fact that had I studied a little harder in school, I might have been there collecting my wings with the rest of the successful cadets. But Camp Blanding was so big, and the seventeen-week basic infantry training so different from what I'd experienced before, that I soon stopped thinking about my former life as a potential pilot.

Like all the other foot soldiers in the infantry, I was now a dogface—a title that accurately summed up our status. Like a pack of stray, nameless canines, my fellow soldiers and I spent much of our time with our faces in the earth. Whether we were frantically digging foxholes or crawling on our bellies beneath barbed wire while machine guns sprayed live ammunition a foot or so above our heads, we were getting accustomed to the feel, smell, and taste of the soil. For many of us, the earth would be the only protection we could rely on. And for some, the ground would soon become our final resting place.

My previous experience with guns was limited. Very limited. When I was just a boy, a friend had once handed me a shotgun, pointed to a rabbit, and told me to take a shot. I did, but the rabbit escaped unscathed, and my shoulder ached as though the bullet had come out the wrong end. Throwing down the weapon, I declared my immediate and irreversible dislike of firearms. I stuck by my word, and I'd never touched another weapon—not even while in the V-5 program, since I'd washed out while the training was still in the pre-combat phase.

Not being a gun man, I found basic training something of a shock. During the seventeen weeks, we were introduced to every weapon we might possibly have to handle. There were machine guns, rifles, mortars, Browning automatic rifles, bazookas that would take out tank treads, and rifle grenades with a kick so fierce we had to use tree trunks for support.

With our shovels always hanging from our backs, we were on constant alert for the order to "dig in!" As soon as those two words filled the air, the shovels blurred into action as we scraped away just enough earth to hide from the enemy's sights and—hopefully—their weapons.

Digging in soil was one thing, but creating a foxhole in the sand was another matter altogether. The war had already spread across three continents, covering terrain that ranged from tropical beaches to mountainous ravines, and we soldiers had to be ready for anything. To make sure we were prepared, our maneuvers were occasionally tested by tanks. Lying in our freshly dug foxholes, trying to catch our breath, we would experience firsthand the volume and force of a thirty-ton Sherman tank as it rolled past, five feet from our heads. If we were lucky, the tanks wouldn't come close enough to cause the foxhole to collapse, but there were no guarantees.

All of us entered the Army at the rank of private, the lowest of the low. There was a clear structure above us, but at Camp Blanding, there was one rank that mattered more than most. Our training was overseen by commissioned

officers, and among them there was a second lieutenant who was hell-bent on pushing our platoon farther
and harder than any other. He marched us longer, made
us climb faster, and fired the machine gun closer to our
heads as we crawled beneath the wire. Nobody respected
Lieutenant Jerk.

Misery and discomfort were not limited to just the
training ground. My infantryman's uniform seemed to be
made of rougher material than the cadet's uniform, and the
food was every bit as bland as I'd feared it would be. Meals
were an unimaginative stream of beans and Spam slopped
onto dented metal trays. The only good thing we dogfaces
got to eat were the glazed donuts that were always served
after a night march.

It was after one of these marches that I returned to my
barracks, tired and looking forward to lying on my cot for
an hour or two before the Florida sun made the air too
hot and stuffy to stay inside. I reached into my trunk to
retrieve my Bible and froze as soon as I opened it. Instead
of the usual neat piles of books, clothes, and other personal
items, the trunk was a mess. It looked as if someone
had rummaged through it at great speed. I immediately
checked for the envelope with $25 I'd stashed inside a sock.
It was gone.

I immediately had a hunch who might have taken the
money. Other people had lost cash from their trunks, and
everyone suspected a shady-looking guy who was often
seen hanging around places he shouldn't have been. Of

course, there was nothing I could do, but I wrote to Bud to let off steam. It was a short letter that got straight to the point.

> Bud, I know you're a captain now, but I've got to tell ya that being in the infantry is the worst thing that could possibly happen to a guy. Even your fellow soldiers will steal $25 and not feel bad about it.

Sending the letter made me feel only slightly better. A little more than a week later, I received a reply from Bud that had a profound impact on me.

> Ray, you're with good men there, and the infantry is the best outfit in the Army. I don't ever want to hear of you saying anything like that again, do you understand? Your loving brother, Bud

I sighed as I read it. I knew my brother was right. I kept reading.

> P.S. Enclosed you'll find $25.

I didn't realize it at the time, but receiving that letter from Bud turned out to be a pivotal moment for me. It did nothing to change the roughness of my uniform, the quality of the food, or the screams of Lieutenant Jerk as he pushed us again and again to outdo all the other platoons.

But it changed how I felt. With a handful of words—and a fistful of dollars—Bud reminded me of the importance of perspective.

Twenty-two years of life had taught me that the way I saw the world would determine how I experienced it. My mom could have seen those hoboes in the backyard as a threat and sent them away. Instead, she saw them as God-given opportunities to act generously. Goffie could have seen her neighbors' overcrowded home as a nuisance, but she chose to view the situation as a chance to help. And I guess I could have considered those daily journeys to Howard's hospital bed as an unwanted distraction from fun and friends, yet I knew visiting him was my duty.

For me, as for so many others of my generation, duty was not a word to be avoided, frowned upon, or belittled. Duty was right and good. Duty was worth dying for. Perhaps that's why the fear had been building in me ever since I had begun my infantry training: I knew there was no backing out.

Being a pilot carried with it a certain sense of invincibility, but with life in the Army, there were no illusions. In the Army, war was real and raw and dangerous—no matter where I ended up. How would I survive? How would I cope?

But perhaps I didn't have to know all the answers. Perhaps it was enough to simply be willing.

With Bud's words firing me up, I resolved to serve and refused to give in to resentment. I was a Christian. I was a free American. And I would pay the price if I had to.

Once again I returned to Joshua, whose story had been a source of inspiration for me since the war began.

Have not I commanded thee? Be strong and of a good courage; be not afraid, neither be thou dismayed: for the LORD thy God is with thee whithersoever thou goest.   JOSHUA 1:9

With my perspective refreshed, I set my mind to completing the final weeks of the training. I still had to deal with the same drills, the same foxholes, and the same shouts, but there was no longer a need for me to resist. With God on my side, I decided I would take whichever path the journey laid out before me.

Then, in the final days of training, I was informed that I wouldn't be leaving with the rest of my platoon but would instead be staying back for six more weeks. I'd serve as acting corporal, assisting with the training of a new batch of enlisted men. I chose to trust that this, too, was part of God's divine plan.

As my platoon headed to Europe in February 1944, I was grateful for another six weeks in the Florida sun. I was fitter than ever, and I found that I enjoyed training the new men. Drills were second nature to me by now, and even weapons training had gotten easier. Life as a corporal couldn't match life as a cadet, but I was done comparing my present situation with a life that no longer existed. There was no time for that.

When the first phase of training was over, I found myself standing at attention before a superior officer.

"Whipps," the officer said, "you're ready to go over. You'll have a short furlough in England, and then you'll be deployed."

I was relieved. I'd never liked the idea of being sent to the South Pacific, with its expanse of islands and the slow fighting in an oppressive climate. I recalled the stories that Uncle Daniels had told me as a child and drew comfort from them. Europe was what I knew. Europe was where men went to fight and returned with stories to tell.

There were just five days to spend at home before shipping out from Camp Kilmer in New Jersey, and I passed the time at East Maynard Avenue visiting with relatives and friends. They were good and happy days, but with every sunset came a growing sense of tension, like a tank moving slowly toward a hastily dug foxhole.

There was no avoiding the inevitable, and eventually I stood outside the Columbus train station wearing my stiff uniform, with my full duffel bag at my side. My mother held me close, tears filling her eyes. I looked at my father. I'd never seen him cry before, but he could no longer hold back the emotion.

Taking a breath to compose himself, my father spoke. "We'll be praying for you regularly, just like we've been praying for your brothers."

Part of me wanted to stay in Columbus and never leave. I wanted to wait for springtime as it woke up the tall trees lining the Olentangy River. I wanted to climb up wide-limbed branches and watch the sky with innocent eyes. But those days were gone.

"Goodbye, Mother. Goodbye, Father." I recognized the voice as my own, and I felt myself pulling away and turning toward the train. It was time to go.

Liverpool, England
September 3, 1944

Dear Mom and Dad,

We left America eleven days ago and arrived in England
yesterday, and already I feel like so much has happened!

One thing I'm learning about Army life is that you have
to expect the unexpected. When we were about to board the
ship, some of the girls told me that each of us had to take a
hammer with us. I thought it was a joke, but it turned out
that every nurse making the crossing needed one. That led
to a frantic search on my last afternoon, and by the time
I'd found a hardware store, it was almost closing time. The
owner was kind and kept the store open for me, and after
listening to my story, he handed me a hammer. He wouldn't
even take money for it!

Life on the ship was so different from what I'd expected.
I don't know why, but I guess I imagined that our ship would
be sailing across the ocean on its own. Every time I went up
on deck and looked out, it seemed as though all I could see
were other ships. We sailed in a pack, and there was never a
time when I couldn't see a cluster of destroyers and aircraft
carriers, all painted the same lead color.

Life below deck was different from what I'd imagined too.
The enlisted men were crammed in like sardines, while the
officers—including us nurses—were only four to a cabin and
had our own lounge. We even got better food than the others.
It bothered me, so some of the other girls and I would fill our
helmets with the afternoon pastries and take them down to
the GIs.

The crew didn't mind us giving away the cakes, but they
did give us a hard time about it. Even before we started
bringing treats for the GIs, they said they'd never seen nurses
eat so much. I'm surprised how hungry I've been—I must
have gained six pounds by now! Even so, I never could bring
myself to join the crew to eat fish for breakfast. That must be

a British tradition (did I mention we were on a British ship?), but that was one new experience too many.

All this talk of food reminds me: Do you remember what the Navy told me when I applied to be a nurse? They were convinced that my overbite meant I would be prone to seasickness. Well, it turned out they couldn't have been more wrong. I was fine all the way over!

Actually, there were a lot of things I didn't need to worry about. A few of the girls were scared we'd get attacked by a German sub on the way over, but the whole ten days passed without incident. We did have to be careful, though. We had heavy sheets draped over the doorways, and if we went out on deck at night, we had to make sure we didn't let the light give away our position.

We finally arrived yesterday. England is, as the locals would say, rather lovely. There's only one thing I can't begin to understand, and that's their money. I have no idea what a shilling is or how many farthings make a penny. Someone on the ship told me there's a coin called a "two-bob bit," but I think he was joking.

The people here smile and wave at us, and the countryside is beautiful. I experienced my first air raid last night, and although I didn't hear any bombs, I don't have to look hard to see bomb damage in the city. I wonder whether we would still be smiling and waving at home if we'd endured so many years of bombs falling on our homes, hospitals, and factories.

Over the last few months, I've spent a lot of time thinking about the soldiers. There was one I treated back in training whose body was covered in burns. His skin looked as if it had been torn away from his body. Even his face was covered in bandages, and all he could do was drink through a straw. Some of the nurses found it hard to treat him, but somehow God gave me the compassion I needed. And I know that's just a glimpse of the things I'll see over here. But by God's grace, I think I am ready.

Mom, Dad, it feels wonderful to finally be on my way to doing something useful. Not a single day has passed since the attack on Pearl Harbor when I haven't prayed that God would let me get out and do what I can to help. I've never wanted to hide from this war—not once. And now that we're here, I'm excited about where I'm going to end up. Back in America, I was so afraid I'd get stuck close to home, but at least I'm in Europe now, just waiting to be assigned to a division. My prayer is that I end up in a field hospital somewhere. I want to be close to the fighting. I want to be able to help.

I've been reading my Bible whenever I have the chance. The seventy-third psalm is the one I keep returning to. "My flesh and my heart faileth: but God is the strength of my heart, and my portion for ever."

That's my prayer—not just for me, but for all of us.

Love,
Betty

5

BREAKFAST FIRST,
THEN BULLETS

AFTER TAKING A TWO-DAY TRAIN RIDE to New Jersey and
then embarking on an eleven-day journey across the Atlantic,
I found myself in Southampton, England, waiting out the
hours before a horde of other men and I were to be shipped
out to France. Some of the guys had slept as they lay on the
floor of the dockside warehouse, but for most of us, sleep was
out of the question. There was far too much to worry about.

Almost since the start of the war, people had been
talking about the Germans' artillery. Exotic and frightening
in equal measure, their weapons represented the struggle
for technological advantage in the war. I'd heard stories
about doodlebugs—remote-controlled tanks the size of

a kid's wagon—that were driven right up to tanks and bridges, where they exploded on impact. Then there was the Fritz X radio-controlled bomb, which was terrorizing vulnerable ships on the ocean, and the Gustav railway gun, which fired eleven-thousand-pound shells during the Siege of Sevastopol, destroying an ammunitions dump hidden behind one hundred feet of rock.

Yet it wasn't any of these weapons that kept me awake. Instead, I'd been thinking about the 88s. These howitzers could take out a plane as it flew overhead, and they were able to destroy a tank from up to nine miles away. And when the Germans turned their sights on Allied troops, firing fifteen to twenty rounds per minute, the results were devastating. If you got caught in an attack from this kind of artillery, there was nothing you could do besides force yourself deeper into your foxhole and pray.

The darkness that settled on us that night by the dock seemed almost permanent, as if it would never give way to the morning. Yet while the minutes stretched on like hours, my mind raced through a barrage of thoughts. How would I react when I heard an 88 for myself? Would I forget all my training? Would I become overwhelmed by fear and freeze? Would I be hit? And if I was, would death come quickly, or would I live long enough to experience the pain as shrapnel tore its way through my flesh?

Slowing my breathing, I returned to the only thing that ever seemed to help when fear threatened to take me down. I prayed.

"Lord, give me the strength and courage I need for this," I whispered. "I don't want to dishonor You."

Somehow the night passed, and it was time to board the Landing Craft Infantry (LCI)—the low-walled, flat-bottomed boats that would take us across the English Channel to the beaches of northern France. The sea had been rough that day—far rougher than my only other experience on angry waters.

That was back on Lake Erie when I was a boy. My grandfather had taken me out on the water, and though the conditions probably weren't that rough, I remember the wind and waves feeling like a violent squall, which put me off boats for life. My nausea had been one of the major influences on my decision to wash out of the Navy Air Corps to make sure I wouldn't wind up a second-class seaman. This time, however, there was no adult to plead with to make it stop and no prospect of a comforting arm to hold on to as the metal walls rose and fell.

Out on the English Channel, as the boat zigzagged its way across in the hope of avoiding German U-boats, all I could do was hang over the side and let my stomach empty out when the sickness took over and eat prunes when the nausea eased. After only a few minutes, I'd feel my insides start to churn again and I'd be back at the railing, watching the gray-green water billow like storm clouds beneath me.

After two or three hours, the noise of the engines fell away and I looked up to see the low coast of France ahead. On June 6, just one week earlier, 150,000 Allied troops had been deposited on the sands between Cherbourg and Le Havre, establishing five beachheads across a fifty-mile stretch of the Normandy coastline. Among these troops had been the men I'd completed my seventeen-week basic training with at Camp Blanding. How many had made it off the beach? I had no way of knowing.

The front of the boat dropped down as the sound of iron chains being fed through metal teeth shut out all other noise. Once the boat was secured, we pressed out into the cold water that surged at our knees. Stealing a sideways glance as I waded toward the shore, I was awed by the scale of the operation. All around me, ships were unleashing thousands of troops and countless vehicles onto the sand. Welcome to Utah Beach.

Once I was out of the water and had gathered with my division on dry land, a realization struck me. It was far quieter here than I'd imagined. Yes, there was the sound of troops slopping through the water, the thunder of Landing Craft Infantry pulling onto the shore, and the roar of trucks and other vehicles, but it wasn't nearly as loud as it could have been. Though I strained to hear, I couldn't detect the boom of heavy weapons. For the first time in days, I felt a faint wave of relief flow through me.

It was almost noon by the time we landed, and the rest of the day was a strange mix of nerves and boredom. Having moved up from the beach, we were told to wait in a clearing filled with tall wooden poles that had been erected by the Germans to prevent Allied gliders from landing there. I felt more like a kid on a field trip than a soldier about to go into combat.

We had watched and marveled as Operation Overlord played out in front of us. Within the span of about ten weeks, as many as three million troops would land on the beaches and move out to fight. This was the start of the drive to force Hitler back and put an end to the war.

As we waited, I took in the other sights around me. I saw German bunkers whose concrete walls had been torn away. I saw stranded American tanks that had been blackened by fire. There were no bodies to be seen, but the debris alone spoke of the scale of the battle that had taken place just a week earlier.

I wasn't alone in these thoughts, and soon the air was filled with bursts of conversation among the men. They were all shocked and scared, just like me. There was talk of kicking the Krauts all the way to Berlin, of doing what the Brits couldn't do on their own, of being home for Christmas. But beneath the bravado, I could sense the doubt and worry.

I could only shake my head. "How in the world did they manage to do it?"

"And how are we going to get back?" The whispered reply came from a young man next to me.

I remembered the advice I'd heard so many times already. "When you get put with your unit, you just have to watch the men who have been here for a while. Do what they do."

The day wore on until it was too late to have us join our new units at the front line. So once more, I curled up around my duffel bag and tried to think myself to sleep. I tried my best to let the sound of the ocean carry me to my dreams, but it was no use. This was my first night on French soil, my first night at war. Sleep was futile.

My first full day in France started early, and we were quickly marched to what amounted to a large truck stop. Lined up along a wide road were dozens of American trucks, some already loaded with supplies, others filled with soldiers. It wasn't long before I was on one of them.

"Welcome to the Red Ball Express," the driver said before he climbed into the cab and released a plume of foul-smelling diesel fumes in our direction.

The drive was short, but it was long enough for me to figure out how the Red Ball Express worked. Trucks were grouped together in units of five or more, with one jeep at the head of the convoy and another at the rear. The route was marked by short, white pillars painted red at the top— hence the name—and it was full of traffic, all of it from military vehicles. It reminded me of an artery feeding fresh blood to tired muscles.

I'd been fighting back nausea ever since we left England, and now that I was wedged into the back of a cargo truck with thirty other GIs of the Fourth Division, Twenty-Second Infantry, I was struggling to keep my stomach settled. I held tighter to the thin metal ribs along the back of the truck and closed my eyes.

Having been unable to sleep the last two nights, I was exhausted. If it weren't for the engine fumes and the pitching of the truck as it sped along, I could have fallen asleep right there. But who was I kidding? Even if I'd had a cot and blankets and a warm mug of cocoa to drink, I'd still be wide awake.

Taking in my surroundings helped keep my mind off my nausea, fatigue, and deep-seated fear. But after just a few miles, the truck slowed as it came to the outskirts of a small town. US troops were milling around, their dirty uniforms and tired faces making it clear that they weren't newcomers. *How long have they been here?* I wondered. Had they been among the soldiers who had pushed the Germans back from Utah Beach, or had they been here longer? Some of them looked as though they'd spent their entire lives fighting.

After we were dropped off, we watched as the convoy turned around and sped back toward the coast. Once the noise of the engines faded, there was a brief, uneasy silence. And that's when I heard it: the sound of mortars exploding some way off.

I flinched. I had no way of knowing how far away they were, but judging by the way the old-timers didn't even blink, I tried to take a breath of comfort.

"Private First Class Whipps?"

We were being called out and assigned to different

platoons, and I was directed toward a tall soldier who was a little older than I was.

"You're with Lieutenant Sanders. He'll take you up to join your men."

Feeling a little like a lost child in a department store, I listened carefully to Sanders's advice.

"Just watch the guys who have been here since the beginning and do what they do. Get down when they get down; move when they move."

With that introduction, I was taken a little farther along a street to the edge of town, passing buildings that were so badly damaged I couldn't even guess what their original purpose had been. After walking a minute or so, I met up with a group of ten men who were sitting behind a barn eating breakfast. They were talking and laughing, and were it not for the debris surrounding them, the weapons at their feet, and the filthy uniforms on their backs, they could have been out camping in the forests in western Ohio.

I sat down to join them.

"Eat this," Sanders said, handing me a tin containing biscuits, powdered coffee, sugar, and chocolate. I had been eating C rations for the past few days, and I knew not to expect much in the way of flavor.

As we ate, I was introduced to the rest of the men. Everyone was relaxed and the sky overhead was quiet, and it was hard to believe that Germans might be anywhere nearby. I wondered how much farther we'd have to travel before we came in range of the enemy.

"How many miles away are the Germans?" I asked.

"Miles?" Sanders asked. His question was accompanied by smiles and gentle laughter from the rest of the men. "Try about two hundred feet on the other side of this wall."

"I don't understand," I said. "If they're that close, why aren't we fighting?"

"Breakfast," he replied. "Neither side starts fighting until they've eaten breakfast. We mostly stop when it gets dark, and we don't start up again until both sides are ready. It's a regular day job out here."

"But how do you know when the fighting's going to start?"

"Whoever finishes eating first sends over the first mortars. That's when we begin."

This made no sense at all. Not that there was much time to ponder it, because within minutes the air was overtaken by the sound of an explosion a little farther behind us, along the road where I'd been dropped off. From where we were, the noise was dull, but I felt like someone had poured ice water into my veins. The other men scrambled to get their helmets on, readying themselves to fight.

"You just stay close by me, Whipps," Sanders said. "Remember what I told you: keep your head down and move when I say."

Almost as soon as the first German mortar exploded, my fellow soldiers started returning fire. Minute after minute the mortars continued, with the Americans launching more than the Germans. Some of the men near me were firing their Brownings, and I could hear the angry sound of an American machine gun as it spat against the enemy. Then came the words I had heard so many times in training—words that had once signaled the start of a simulated maneuver or a fake raid on a dummy enemy. But we were a long way from Florida now, and the words had acquired a whole new sense of urgency.

The cry came again: "Move out!"

Taking a deliberate breath, I made my way to the edge of the barn. I followed the boots in front of me, picking up the pace as they broke into a run.

I didn't have a clue what to expect once I cleared the barn. When I got my first glimpse beyond the building, the scene was unimpressive. The barn gave way to a field not much longer than a football field, and it had a thick hedge running around it. The ground beneath my feet was covered with overgrown clumps of grass, while a bright-blue sky hung above. It was just a typical European field. Maybe this wouldn't be so terrifying after all.

The first clap of a bullet stunned me as it passed by. I couldn't be sure how close it was, but it was a bullet all right. The sound it made was unmistakable, like a hand being brought down hard onto a solid table. I bent lower and ran faster, not even considering firing back or looking out for the enemy. All I could think about was running, following the standard-issue boots ahead of me as they sped over the grass.

Just as the grass banked up and reached the thick hedge-row on the far side of the field, the pair of feet stopped.

I followed Sanders's lead and lay on the ground, listening
as the soldiers around me resumed firing. In the moment's
pause, I heard myself breathing and noticed that I was praying silently, recalling the final words of my favorite psalm:
*The salvation of the righteous is of the LORD: he is their strength
in the time of trouble.*

Peering over the bank through the dense mass of thorns
and bushes, I glimpsed a man running ahead in the next
field. For a moment, I wondered why one of my colleagues
would have charged ahead when there was no order to
move out. A burst of machine-gun fire came from my left
side and sent me diving behind the bank. When the firing
stopped, I saw that the man—who was wearing a German
uniform—was no longer running in the field. He was lying
facedown in it.

The rest of the day passed in much the same way.
Exchanges would start with mortar fire, machine guns,
and other weapons. At some point we would be given
the order to move out, and we'd climb out from whatever
barrier we'd hidden behind—a foxhole, a natural bank, or a
building—and charge across the field ahead.

At first I saw the Germans only when they were far off
and in retreat, but after a while I learned to join in the
firing. I'd look for the enemy, hold the place in my mind,
and fire several rounds from my M1 rifle as fast as I could
before tucking myself into the safety of the earth.

"Welcome to hedgerow fighting," Sanders said once
the sun had set and I joined the other men opening their

C rations. "There's really not that much more to it than what you saw today. It's slow fighting, just taking one field at a time. On a good day we'll make it across five or six, but sometimes we'll only take three."

There was one part of hedgerow fighting that I didn't see that first day. I had yet to see a casualty among my own men. Unfortunately, I didn't have to wait long.

★

The following day, the routine was already beginning to feel, if not comfortable, at least familiar to me. The men had all been welcoming and friendly, but I'd noticed that of the twelve men in my squad, one of them—Private Bailey—was always set apart. Bailey didn't talk much, and he and I had yet to exchange any words at all.

We'd finished breakfast an hour or so earlier, and the Germans had moved out of their positions from the previous night, vacating the foxholes that had sheltered them from our attack. The men in my squad were crouched in our own foxholes, most of them in pairs. Bailey was alone in his hole when the fight for the next field began with heavy mortar fire.

The sound of the mortar landing so close to me—perhaps just ten feet away—left my ears ringing and caused me to automatically check my limbs for injury.

Then I heard the shout: "Medic! Bailey's hit!"

I was still shadowing Sanders, so I crawled along behind him as he went to see how bad Bailey's injury was.

I looked into the foxhole and saw that Bailey had suffered a direct hit on the torso. His limbs were all intact, but where his uniform had buttoned up his chest, there was now a seeping mass of blood and organs, shattered bone, and torn-up fabric. The smell—a mixture of fireworks and burned hair—made me gag. I turned away as quickly as I could, but there was no hiding from the terror that was tearing my guts to shreds. There was no way to escape this sense of dread. How would I ever make it out alive?

6

HEDGEROW COUNTRY

As I OPENED MY EYES after a night of fitful sleep (if I slept
at all), my body felt as uncertain and as hazy as the early-
morning mist that loitered in the sky above. Inches from
my face were the walls of my foxhole, filling the air with
the smell of damp earth. I didn't remember digging in the
night before, but judging by the state of my hands and my
uniform, I might as well have spent the night in a pigpen.

It doesn't take much experience in the military to
be introduced to a whole new way of waking up in the
morning. From my early days of training with the Navy Air
Corps, I'd learned that waking up slowly was a luxury I could
do without. Experience had taught me that within a couple

of minutes of opening my eyes, I could be running, digging, or standing at attention—fully alert and fully awake.

But this morning there was no sergeant bawling orders, no cot to be made, and no blankets to tidy away. It was just me in my foxhole, a minicrater about three and a half feet deep and three feet across. I was curled up beneath my raincoat, staring at the sky, which was the same Army-issue gray as the battleships that had been lined up in the harbor in Southampton.

I kept still. Was it really possible that only seventy-two hours had passed since I'd been standing in line, waiting to board one of those ships and cross the English Channel to France? Somehow it seemed as though I'd lived three years in those last three days.

I wasn't the only one awake. I could hear voices talking quietly somewhere nearby, and I strained to listen. Were those German voices that I heard? I quickly discounted the idea, but it was too late. Adrenaline had hijacked my heart, and there was no way I could remain still any longer.

Once out of the foxhole, I got my bearings again. We'd taken seven fields the previous day, and we'd dug in a little behind the last hedgerow we'd reached. Even though they were made of nothing more than earth and undergrowth, these hedgerows made formidable defenses. They all looked the same: foundations composed of four-foot-high banks of earth, with angry tangles of thorny bushes growing on top. Most were thick enough that they were nearly impossible to see through. That meant a tank could be hidden behind one of these hedgerows, not to mention a squadron of men. And while these barriers gave a measure of protection to our troops, we knew that they were equally helpful to the Germans. Here in France at least, the earth seemed to be taking no sides in this war.

I joined the other men who had started eating their C rations. They looked old, but not in years. There was a weariness to them—a weathered look I might have expected from the hoboes my mom had fed but not from guys who had just arrived on the battlefield. Apparently one week of fighting had been enough to drain them of more life than I thought possible.

"You landed at Utah?" one soldier asked me.

"Yes."

"How did it look?"

"Not bad," I said. "I thought it would be worse. I guess they've cleaned it up a bit since . . ."

"Utah was never too bad," he said. "The Heinies had been knocked out before, so it didn't take us long to get up off the beach. We had it easy compared to what the boys faced at Omaha."

Breakfast carried on quietly after that. I was among the first wave of replacements, and I wondered how the other guys would take to me. Thankfully, they didn't seem to resent me so far. Even so, I decided to keep quiet for a while and spend more time watching than I did speaking.

We were just finishing breakfast when my ears were filled with the sound of artillery fire. First came the distant slap as the shell was fired up ahead of us, and then came the high whistle as the missile made its way closer to us. It was a terrible sound, as if the air itself were being ripped apart. My instincts kicked in instantly, and I dived facedown into the earth. I closed my eyes and waited for the impact.

The sound went on longer than I expected, and when it finally ended in an explosion that sent tiny tremors through the earth, I could tell the missile had landed some distance behind us. I exhaled in relief. When I looked up, I saw that my breakfast companions were still sitting in their places, digging out forkfuls of ham and chocolate from their ration tins. They were all smiling at me.

"Don't worry, Whipps. You'll work out which ones are coming close soon enough. Until then, just do what we do."

Though they'd missed us by quite a distance, the Germans were clearly awake and ready to fight. It didn't take long before I was crouched beside the other men in my squad, pressing my back against the earth that formed the base of the hedgerow. Though I held tight to my weapon, I let the others take care of the firing. A few men were taking turns trying to pick off the Germans who were hiding at the other end of the field, while a few feet farther along the row, some of our boys were sending M2 mortars over, working in teams of three to feed the shells into the metal tube.

One of the things they couldn't have prepared me for during training was the smell. Somehow it had never occurred to me that war would have such a distinct odor. There's the smell of burned powder that accompanies artillery shells and the unmistakable kick that comes when several rifles are firing all at once. Burned flesh lingers in the air far too long, and the smell of death that follows the loss of blood was one I hoped I'd never encounter again. On that first full day of fighting, I smelled them all.

When the order came for us to move out, I followed the boots in front of me through a gap in the hedge and across the field. We moved as fast as we could, not wanting to remain exposed and vulnerable any longer than necessary. We repeated the same ritual again and again throughout the morning.

At one point I was hunkered down behind the hedgerow with the other guys. Gathering my courage, I pushed myself up and saw that there was a small gap in the tangle of bushes above me—just enough to peer through. I noticed a German soldier a couple of fields ahead, moving through a gap they'd blown to serve as an escape route when they had to fall back. I sighted my M1 the best I could and fired off all eight shots. I didn't look to see if I'd killed him. I didn't need to.

"Move out!" The shout came once again, and I hurled myself across another field. By the time I reached the other side and started firing again, my mind had already moved on from thoughts of the man I'd just shot. It took everything in me to concentrate on staying alive.

Lord, I prayed more times throughout that day than I could keep track of, *give me strength. Keep me safe.*

Within a couple of days, I was no longer holding back when we engaged the enemy. After four or five days, I learned which artillery sounds I could ignore and which ones I needed to dive for. By the end of the first week, I knew I needed to do anything I could to help a wounded colleague. I learned how to pour sulfur on an injury to prevent infection and how to do a basic wrap on a wound. I also learned to use the injured man's medical kit instead of my own. The thinking behind this was that if he was wounded badly enough to need treatment, he could replenish his supplies when he went back down the line. Those of us on the front line didn't know when we'd need the sulfur, morphine, and bandages ourselves.

I learned that some injuries were worse than others. For instance, being shot was preferable to being blasted at close range with shrapnel. The shards of metal contained in the shells would rip through flesh just as easily as they would slice through a uniform.

As the days slipped by and I finished my first week of combat, I had a suspicion that something had changed within me. The fear I'd felt initially—so intense it had threatened to freeze my boots to the ground—no longer had such a firm grip on me. I'd learned to shake off the temptation to cower, statue-like, when fighting was taking place around me.

That's not to say I wasn't scared. The fear stayed with

me all the time, spiking when the 88s came in or the call to move out sounded above the firing. But it was no longer the only thing I felt. As I moved—sometimes running, sometimes crawling—I found that some measure of reassurance and comfort were beginning to seep into me. Feeling scared didn't mean I had to sit and wait for death to find me.

I learned much of this mentality from Lieutenant Sanders. He was the kind of leader who was always in front, always pushing forward to be the first one out from behind the hedgerow. He was the only leader I'd seen combat with so far, but I knew a few of the sergeants back in Camp Blanding would never have led this way. They would have been at the back, sending us dogfaces forward to soak up the worst of the danger before they ventured out.

To his credit, Sanders never bad-mouthed the men who held back. He just kept calling them to follow him, reassuring them in the quiet moments that they'd get it eventually. And they did. Even though the fighting was much more intense than anyone had anticipated, and even though the high turnover of men was a daily reminder that we were losing soldiers at an alarming rate, Sanders never stopped leading his men forward. Deciding to follow him was one of the simplest decisions I ever had to make.

From time to time we'd get a replacement soldier who would want to talk about what to expect and how to cope. But most of them just needed to hear the same words Sanders had told me on my first day: stay close by, keep your head down, and move when we say. There really wasn't much more to it.

As the end of June approached, our progress through hedgerow country remained slow. We were still taking just five or six fields a day, and though we were never in retreat, we'd advanced only a few miles from the coast. If we were going to liberate Paris, it would take forever at this pace.

One of the problems was the fact that the hedgerows were too much for our tanks. Whenever they tried to roll over the four-foot-high banks, the unprotected undersides were left high and exposed, making them easy targets for German artillery. So throughout our first month, our tanks were relegated to country lanes and tracks that ran alongside the fields. They were a little safer there, unless a German spotted them. Either way, they offered us minimal support.

It was sometime around the end of June when we had our first break in the fighting. I woke up the way I usually did, staring at the mud walls of my foxhole. *How will I cope with sleeping outside once summer slips away?* I wondered.

From the moment I got out, though, I sensed that something was different. I looked around, but I couldn't quite put my finger on what it was.

"Do you notice that?" It was a tall private from the South whom we all called Tennessee.

"What is it?" I said.

"Listen." He paused for a few seconds. "No guns."

He was right. Ever since I'd arrived, there had been the continual thunder of artillery in the background. It had become so routine by now that I'd all but blocked it out. Now that Tennessee pointed it out, though, the quiet seemed strange.

"We took Cherbourg," he said.

The rest of the day almost felt like a vacation. We pulled back from the front and lined up for our first hot meal since we'd arrived. It was an unexpected luxury—having time to talk and relax a little. To my surprise, stories about the war began tumbling out. I listened, amazed, as men who had barely uttered a word in the previous weeks spun tale after tale.

The stories had a language all their own. As we waited in the chow line, men talked about going "souvenir hunting" by frisking the bodies of dead Germans. They hoped to find something valuable to take home with them, such as a watch, a knife, or—best of all—a genuine German pistol. Other men talked about "gold bricking," which caught my attention more than the stories about the souvenirs. Gold brickers were the soldiers who were so desperate to get away from the front lines that they would feign some kind of illness.

"How could you fake something serious enough to get you sent back?" I asked the private first class who seemed to know the most about it all.

"Some guys pretend the fighting is making them crazy

and they've got shell shock. They hope that someone will send them home with the rest of the Section Eights."

"Oh." The thought never would have occurred to me.

"But that don't work so good. If you really want to get sent home, you've got to get shot. I've seen people take off their boot and hold a foot up out of the foxhole, waving it around hoping some Kraut's got good enough aim to hit it."

"Yeah," another solder said, "I've heard some guys will shoot their feet themselves if they're desperate enough."

It didn't make sense to me. I understood the fear, but I couldn't imagine feeling so desperate that I'd shoot myself to escape. Since I'd arrived in France, my New Testament had left my breast pocket only when I took it out to read it during lulls in the fighting. The more I returned to it, the more I knew how dependent I was on God for everything I needed to survive the war.

My constant prayer had changed, and now in addition to asking God to give me strength and safety, I was also asking Him to give me courage. I couldn't imagine fighting in this war without the hope of some God-given valor to draw on. Not that I was better than any other soldier or that God was looking out for me more than anyone else. I just knew that my survival was not in my own hands.

The boost of pushing the Germans out of Cherbourg was short lived. The next day we were back to the hedgerows, and once again we inched our way forward, field by field. Between the slow progress we were making and the high turnover of men, it didn't take long for morale to drop again. The Germans we were fighting looked a little different too. As we pressed inland, I noticed that the dead Germans we passed were getting younger.

"They put the old troops at the front," Sanders explained when I asked him about it. "Now we're getting to the SS. They're a lot harder to kill."

He was right. We also had to watch out for snipers hiding in tall buildings and trees. Our only choice was to draw fire from them in the hope that by giving away their position, we could take them out before they struck one of our men.

Early in July, we had a breakthrough. Someone figured out that if the tanks were fitted with a kind of metal snowplow at the front, they could carve right through the hedgerows. It had taken a while to create the best design, but eventually we started to see our M4 Sherman tanks and M3 Stuart tanks fitted with strange-looking metal teeth on the front. Once they were back in the fields leading the way, our advance accelerated drastically.

Amid the successes, however, we also faced some significant setbacks. Late one afternoon Sanders called me over.

"Whipps," he said, "I think there's a squad of Germans on the other side of those trees. I want you to go with the sergeant and get them."

Tennessee joined the sergeant and me, along with a

couple of the newer guys who were doing well. We moved as quickly as we could without giving ourselves away, heading down a track that was lined with tall hedgerows on each side. A couple of hundred feet in, we cut back into the field and tracked along the hedgerow as it ran alongside a small clump of trees.

I hadn't done anything like this since arriving in France, but it was the kind of maneuver we'd practiced frequently during training. I tried to remember the things I'd learned: stay low, keep alert, maintain the right distance between the other men and me. My heart was pumping wildly, but I reminded myself to breathe and not let fear overrule my courage. And I prayed. I prayed with every step.

We heard the Germans before we saw them. I didn't speak the language, but I could tell it was the easy chatter of men who were relaxed. The sergeant must have been thinking the same thing, because he slowed his pace. What if it was a trick? What if the trees held a sniper who was just waiting until we got close enough to be picked off? I scanned the trees the best I could. Seeing nothing, we moved forward, the sergeant in the lead. I followed every step carefully, hoping I wouldn't make a sound.

I didn't know what I was expecting to see when we finally rounded the gap in the hedgerow. I certainly didn't expect to see six German soldiers sitting down with a meal spread out in front of them, their weapons stacked up in a pyramid a couple of paces away. In that moment

I froze, halted by a single question: Could I really kill unarmed men?

The sergeant nodded, and Tennessee and the others opened fire without me. I stood there, paralyzed. A couple of the Germans made it to their weapons and returned fire, but within seconds, the exchange was over. They were all dead. I'd been gripped by buck fever and hadn't fired a shot.

I looked back and saw that Tennessee was lying down. His helmet was off and his hair was matted with blood.

Guilt and sorrow such as I'd never felt before flooded over me. My hesitation had played a part in all this. I watched the other men attending to Tennessee, then turned back and scanned for more Germans. But it was too late. They were all dead. And so was Tennessee.

7

BREAKTHROUGH

THE FIRST TIME I HEARD SOMEONE SAY IT, I thought it was just another one of those wild rumors that make up the fabric of Army life. I brushed it off the second time too. But by the third time, I was starting to believe there might be something to it.

"Patton's going to make a push for Paris," a clean-cut private said as he sat down to eat with me and a group of other soldiers. We had time to kill that afternoon, waiting for our next orders. "He says he's going to get there in sixteen days."

Everybody knew about General Patton. Old Blood and Guts, he was called, and almost every time that nickname was mentioned, you didn't have to wait long before another soldier would follow up with this explanation: "Yup, his guts and your blood." Patton was a force of nature, having led successfully in North Africa as well as Sicily. If he was coming to France, it had to mean good news for us.

But sixteen days? In the month since our boys had landed on the stretch of Normandy coastline that ran from Cherbourg in the west almost to Le Havre in the east, we'd made it only as far south as the town of Saint-Lô. We'd fought hard for every field and lost so many men that I could no longer keep track of the names of the replacements. And after all that blood and guts, we were still only twenty miles from the coast. Paris was almost ten times as far away. How on earth could we reach it so quickly? Then again, if anyone could, it was Patton.

"I heard about him in Sicily." The private paused in the middle of a bite. "He was visiting some wounded GIs, and when he saw one who didn't have any bandages on him, he asked what was wrong. This fella said he was exhausted and couldn't take it. Well, Old Blood and Guts wasn't having none of that, so he slapped him on the face and called him a coward. Then he dragged him out of the tent and told him to go back to the front line." The private laughed when he got to this bit. No one else did. "Maybe if he comes here, we won't see so many gold brickers. Huh, fellas?"

Nobody spoke; we just watched as the private returned to his tin. But we were thinking the same thing. Our minds

were swirling with thoughts of fear and death and the fact
that there was a coward inside each of us. There was a
warrior, too—someone who fought with courage in spite of
the fear—but that coward within could shout pretty loudly
at times.

I watched the private finish his chow. *How long will it be
before he hears his inner coward?* I wondered.

The rumors about Patton carried on for days, but meanwhile there was still fighting to be done. We had pushed
the Germans back to Saint-Lô, but there were still enemy
pockets in town that we needed to clear. Our fighting
shifted from the farmers' fields and country lanes to tightly
packed-in streets and buildings. This kind of fighting was
unfamiliar and strange, and I didn't like it at all. Even
pausing to fix the bayonet onto the front of my rifle made
me nervous. At least with hedgerow fighting, you could be
sure that the enemy was in front of you and that most of
the time they were one or two hundred feet away. In town,
it was different. Every street corner, every edge of a building, every window, and every burned-out tank was a potential hiding place for the Germans.

Lord, I prayed as I moved out from behind a house one
day, *please keep me safe.*

Along with two others, I had to run across a patch of
grass the width of a football field to a building on the other
side. Other men in my squad laid down covering fire,

forcing the Germans to hide for a few seconds while we made our way across. By this time I had run across enough fields to know that I no longer needed to follow the pair of boots ahead of me, and I looked up as I ran, making sure the way was clear.

Keep me safe, Lord, I prayed silently as I ran, my eyes stealing quick glances around me.

With only twenty feet to go, I looked left and saw the unmistakable shape of a German helmet ducking behind a fence about thirty feet away. I had no time to think or even react, because as soon as I had registered the soldier, the air was filled with the unmistakable crack of German artillery.

I couldn't tell you if it was an 88 or a smaller mortar. I couldn't even tell you if I tripped or if I threw myself to the ground. All I know is that the moment the shell exploded, I was facedown on hard earth, my hands pulling my helmet tightly over my head. Another shell exploded, then another. I stayed where I was, willing myself farther into the ground. I heard our boys return fire from behind me; then there was silence.

My hands were stinging. I inched myself up enough to get a look at them. They were covered in blood. I felt a little sickened at the sight, but I'd seen far worse injuries on other men. The call to move on told me it was safe to get up and make the last twenty feet across the open space to the next building, and when I got there, I showed my injury to the sergeant.

"You're going to have to get that looked at, Whipps,"

he said with a shrug. "Go back down and have the medics clean out the shrapnel."

It was only as I snaked my way back to the company base that I realized my back was stinging too, but I figured that since I could still walk unaided, any shrapnel in my back couldn't cause too much trouble. By the time I arrived at the medics' station, I wasn't worried, but the pain in my hands was starting to get uncomfortable.

"This is a good one," the medic said. "You'll get five points and a Purple Heart for this, soldier."

That made me happy. I didn't care about the medal, but the points were valuable. Points were awarded for length of service, for showing exceptional courage, for taking part in a particular battle, and for getting injured. Once we reached eighty-five points, we'd get sent home.

I rested happily for a few hours, feeling grateful to God yet again for keeping me safe, and thankful that I was now one step closer to getting sent home. I'd never planned on getting a bunch of points from injuries, but if I was going to get hurt, this was the way to do it. By the end of the day, I was reporting back to my sergeant, my hands bandaged up too much for me to be of use with a rifle for a few days.

By the time my hands had healed, Saint-Lô had fallen. In the break that followed, we found out that the rumors about General Patton were true: he really was going to lead the push for Paris. And then came the even better news: he was taking the Fourth Division, Twenty-Second Infantry with him. We'd be riding with his convoy of tanks, half-tracks, and trucks as he pushed the Germans back at such a pace that they wouldn't know what had hit them. And if the riflemen of the Twenty-Second Infantry ever got in trouble, they'd have a little extra support on the ground.

In the three days before the new campaign was to start, we spent much of our time resting. Men did what soldiers always do when they have time on their hands: they played dice or backgammon or just griped about all the bad decisions the generals had been making. There were thousands of us soldiers in Saint-Lô, crowding every bombed-out corner and every rubble-strewn road. I didn't know what to be more impressed by, the scale of the devastation or the number of forces that were being prepared to catapult east.

My squad was assigned to one particular tank unit. Like all tankers, they were a close-knit group that relied on one another to do their jobs. But they were happy enough to take us with them, as long as we stayed out of the tank, held on tight, and didn't fall off.

One morning while we were waiting for our next orders, Lieutenant Sanders told me to report to the company commander. I had no idea what to expect, and I hadn't had a lot of time to mull over my performance up to this point. I supposed I'd fought well enough, although Tennessee's death still weighed heavily on me.

I found the commander in a broken-down building that

must have been a school at some point. The ceilings were high, and the windows were all blown out.

"Private First Class Whipps?" he said.

"Yes, sir."

"Since you're coming with us to Paris, I want you to be our company radio man."

I was pleased. Being with the company meant I'd be removed from the action a bit, and being a radio man meant I'd be sticking by my officer and relaying any information he gave me back to the captain. Carrying a thirty-five-pound radio on my back would be a small price to pay.

"Yes, sir," I said before being dismissed.

As we moved out with the rest of General Patton's Third Army, the fighting we were engaged in was only sporadic, and with the tanks not going much faster than thirty miles an hour, I felt the safest I had in some time. As I crouched on top and held on to the metal, I watched the French countryside wash by.

Almost immediately, I started to see things I hadn't noticed before. Up to this point, I'd been aware of only the soldiers—either allies or enemies—but as our convoy of iron and gasoline headed east, I noticed that we weren't the only people around. Among the rubble of shattered buildings and burned-out houses, I saw mostly women, but also some old men and young children. Sometimes they'd stop and wave at us, the children calling out for bonbons and "sha-co-lat," the adults clutching tightly to whatever valuables they were able to carry. It had been four years since these people had lost their freedom, and some of them looked so frail I marveled that they'd made it through alive.

The fighting carried on. We came across occasional squads of Germans from time to time, and more than one tank unit. But our numbers and firepower meant that we never had to pause our advance for more than a day.

Traveling on tanks changed the way I saw the enemy, too. On the few occasions when I'd seen German panzer tanks during the hedgerow fighting, I'd been in awe of them. They were bigger and louder than our Shermans—another symbol of the German army's firepower. But riding with our tank guys helped me to see them differently, to identify their weaknesses and think about how to get to the crew inside rather than worrying about the potential damage their guns could inflict. I learned that it was possible to hide from their view, to disable their tracks, and to pick them off when they opened their tank lids to come out.

Sleep came easily in those days. There were so many of us traveling that there wasn't space to dig foxholes at night, so we just took off our boots and lay down on the ground. Every morning we'd have to tip our boots upside down and shake out any small lizards that had crawled in, but they were harmless enough.

About the worst thing we had to face on a regular basis was guard duty. It was a vital job, and we took turns staying awake for several hours every few nights. Some men could make themselves stay awake even if they were sitting still, but not me. I had to be up and moving. I kept alert by focusing on the tanks that lay dotted across the landscape, spread like ancient stepping stones across a dark gray sea.

That's what I was doing when I heard the planes. It wasn't late—maybe about ten o'clock—so most of the rest of the guys heard them too. There was nothing we could do but wait and listen. The deep, low noise was easy to ignore at first, but it grew louder with each second that passed. Soon it was the only sound we could hear, drowning out the soldiers' cussing as they fixed their eyes overhead.

"Oh boy," I said as a group of bombers came into view.

All eyes were on the planes as they came right over us. Then came bursts of light—bright yellow, almost white—that lit up the underside of their wings, revealing the familiar black cross that marked them as Luftwaffe.

We scanned the sky, but no bombs fell. The flares continued to drop, lighting up the sky as they sank to the ground.

"Either they're taking photographs or they're getting ready to come back and bomb us," one of the tank crewmen said. "Either way, there's not much we can do now."

The smell of the magnesium flares lingered for what felt like hours, and that night, sleep didn't come easily. No matter how hard I tried, I couldn't stop myself from imagining that the faintest sound was the start of a return attack. But the attack never came.

★

We made significant progress as the days went by—more than any of us thought possible. The farther we went, the harder it was to keep up our supplies, but that didn't stop General Patton. He was charging toward Paris with the zeal of a man on a mission, and word started to get around that his sixteen-day prediction wasn't so crazy after all.

One morning, we were making good time along roads that wove through the flat landscape. Our tanks were separated by the usual fifty-foot gap, and at one point I noticed that the men on the tank ahead were staring into the sky behind us. I followed their gaze, and I saw a group of our planes heading straight for us.

My time in the Navy Air Corps had involved plenty of study of various planes, and I recognized these right away as our P-47 fighters. They weren't an unusual sight in themselves, but the way they were flying looked ominous. They were coming in fast and low—not much higher than fifty feet. It was obvious they were coming in to attack, and although the tank was still moving ahead, everybody jumped to the ground. I made the seven-foot drop without hurting myself, even with the extra weight of the radio on my back. I'd had no idea back when I was throwing my body through the obstacle course in Gonzaga how useful that training would end up being one day.

"Get out the tarp!" called one of the sergeants.

Two men scrambled to unfold the bright orange tarp

that was designed to show aircraft that we were US Army. They hauled it out behind us, but the P-47s kept coming. Hugging the ground, the planes started firing, unleashing a string of bullets that traced the lines of our tanks, starting hundreds of feet behind us. By now the Sherman had come to a stop, and I tucked myself beneath the tracks, hoping that between the tank, its tracks, and my radio I would be as well covered as possible.

Every muscle within me clenched as I heard the planes roar overhead. All three of them passed by, bullets stinging the ground around us, the sound of metal on metal coming from farther ahead.

The attack was over as soon as it began, and immediately my officer was shouting into the radio, "What's the Air Force thinking? We've just been strafed out here!"

Before we moved out again, news came from the tank ahead of us.

I picked up my radio and called in the message: "We lost a man in that attack."

I put down the receiver and waited, though not for anything in particular. There was a heaviness about the silence, and all I could do was force myself to sit and breathe awhile.

By the time we reached the outskirts of Paris, the friendly fire incident was put behind us. There was a city to liberate and people who were counting on us. Yet while Patton's men of the Third Army rode through the streets lined with people cheering in French, I was among those who were diverted north. While thousands of American soldiers drank wine and saw the city sights, I was camped in a farmer's field an hour outside the city center. But these accommodations suited me fine. I was too tired to do anything more than sleep and rest anyway.

I spoke enough French that I was made the company spokesman. I explained to the farmer who owned the land that we needed to dig foxholes and wait here for a few days.

"Do anything you like," he said. "We're just grateful you are here."

And so, as the last days of August slipped away, we waited.

During my two and a half months in France, I'd been awarded a Purple Heart, I'd been shot at by my own fighter planes, and I'd watched too many of my own men die. I'd seen Germans surrender, and I'd seen Germans fight to the death. I'd learned to make myself move even when fear threatened to root me to the spot, and I'd learned to do as I was ordered—and do it well. I'd learned to sleep even though danger might lie less than a mile away and to fire my rifle even though I detested the death it unleashed.

Most of all, though, I'd learned that if anything was going to get me through this war, it was my faith in God. That didn't mean I was a pacifist, nor did it make me immune to the sights, sounds, and smells of death. But God taught me a simple lesson during those hard days of fighting and those long nights in foxholes—the same lesson He'd taught one of the greatest warriors in history. He taught me about courage.

The Bible I had with me contained only the New Testament and the Psalms, but there was a passage from the Old Testament that I'd memorized years before: "Have not I commanded thee? Be strong and of a good courage; be not afraid, neither be thou dismayed: for the LORD thy God is with thee whithersoever thou goest" (Joshua 1:9).

There was not a day that went by when I didn't think about those words. I believed that just as God had commanded Joshua, He also commanded me. Instead of giving in to fear or allowing my thoughts to succumb to bleakness and worry, I could choose to be strong and courageous. Courage was possible because of one simple truth: there was not a single moment of this war when I was alone.

In every foxhole and every field, I was not alone. In every moment when the smells and sights of death filled my senses, I was not alone. In every moment when the air was filled with the sounds of bullets and mortar shells and fighter planes, I was not alone. In all of this, God was with me. Wherever I went, the Lord my God was there too.

167th General Hospital
Cherbourg, France

September 18, 1944

Dear Mom and Dad,

It's hard to believe that over a week has passed since we arrived in France. I feel bad for not writing to you before now, but the truth is, there really hasn't been a moment to stop. Even though we're a long way from the fighting, they're keeping us busy out here.

The crossing over the English Channel was exciting. Well, it was for me, at least. We were in small boats called LCIs, and it was pretty choppy. While almost everyone else was suffering with terrible seasickness, I felt just fine! I spent much of the crossing to France eating K rations with the one fellow on board who hadn't turned green. So much for the Navy's theory about my overbite!

As you know, I wanted to be sent to a station hospital—one that was close to the line, where the men really need help. Well, the 167th General Hospital isn't like that. We're set about as far away from the front as it's possible to be in France. So you don't need to worry about me. I'm just as safe here as I was at home.

The hospital here is vast. There are 1,500 beds and a huge staff of doctors, nurses, orderlies, and probably some other people I've never even seen yet. I'm on Ward B, where the men come after they've had surgery. We look after them for a maximum of thirty days—no more. After that, either they go back to fight or they're sent to England for further recovery.

In some ways it all feels so normal. I spend every moment of my shifts checking on the men in the five tents I'm responsible for. With more than one hundred beds between them, that means there's no time to stop and think about being away from home or being at war. And there's certainly no time to get bored.

Life here is a lot different from home. We get half a helmet of water each day to wash in, and we don't dare throw it away, because some days we don't get any water at all. We work seven days a week, twelve hours a day. But I don't feel deprived or mistreated. This is how I can help, and I'm just glad to do my part.

I sleep on a little cot in a tent with three other girls: Dora Clark, Peggy Clark (same name but not related), and Ruth Brown. Dora is a little older than the rest of us. She used to be married to a doctor—she put him through law school and then through medical school, and then he dumped her when they both joined the service. She's just a jewel. I can't imagine why anyone would treat her so badly. Peggy is from Seattle. She's beautiful and fun, too. Ruth's Canadian. All of us get on so well.

By the way, there's one thing here that's not so great. We don't have any toilet paper! All the girls are writing to their folks back home and asking for some for Christmas. If you could send me some as my present, I'd be so thankful. Don't bother with wrapping it, though!

The work on the wards isn't too hard. A lot of the men have shrapnel wounds, but the doctors are good at sewing them up. One of the most important things for us nurses to do is to watch out for infection. We try to keep the men happy, too, and even though they've only been in France since the summer, a lot of them have that look in their eyes that tells you they've been through some horrible experiences already.

We mustn't get too friendly, though. We've been told by Major Leonard, the nurse who's in charge of all of us, that under no circumstances are we to fraternize with the enlisted men. "You're officers—remember that, girls." They don't mind if a girl goes on a date with a married man, just as long as he's an officer, too. It's another one of those things that I just don't get about the Army.

I've been going to church every Sunday I'm not on duty. The chaplain's a Unitarian minister, and I haven't really enjoyed his services so far. He seems to talk about anything but the Lord. The real problem is that even though he has a wife and two children at home, out here he dates single nurses.

Even if church isn't quite what it is back home, I've found time to read my Bible. There are a lot of other Christian nurses here, though I haven't met many men who are. Even though we're not in any real danger out here, we know we need to hold on to our faith in order to get through. And I think God really is listening and helping us. Somehow we've all had enough energy to keep going this week, and for that I'm thankful.

Whatever happens, I want what I do to count. I want to serve. I want to be faithful and do my part well. This isn't where I thought I'd end up, but I trust that God has put me here for a reason.

I hope that you are well and that life is good back home. Write back and tell me all the news. I want to know everything!

With love to you and the boys, too,

Betty

8

OVER BY CHRISTMAS

WE WERE SOME THIRTY MILES OUTSIDE PARIS, facing another day, another food line. I looked down at my boots and struggled to tell what was dried-on mud and what was the original leather. When was the last time I'd cleaned them? For that matter, when had I last cleaned myself, let alone soaked in a tub or slept on a mattress? No matter how hard I tried, I found it impossible to figure out how many days had slipped by since I'd been in civilization. Six months? I was pretty sure that was how long it had been since I'd sailed across the Atlantic, but half a year sounded too short. How could I have seen so much in such a short space of time?

The line shuffled forward slowly. I was waiting for new food rations, but now that September was halfway over, I was really hoping to pick up some winter clothing. Since landing in Normandy three months earlier, it hadn't been too cold at night yet, but I didn't like the idea of pushing farther north with just my raincoat for extra warmth.

Reaching the front of the line, I saw that they were handing out only food. I paused at the base of the truck long enough for the soldier in the rear to read my mind.

"This war's going to be over by Christmas," he said. "You're not going to need no winter clothes."

I was not encouraged.

It was true that we were moving rapidly. Those early days we had spent inching our way across the fields of Normandy seemed like a decade ago. Riding with Patton's boys of the Third Army was so much faster, and after rolling around Paris for a few days at the end of August, we packed up and pushed north to Belgium. Even though we'd left Patton and his tanks and rejoined the rest of the Fourth Division, we were still advancing rapidly. Day by day, the miles fell away behind us.

But all that speed and all the territory we were regaining came at a price. We needed a constant supply of new troops, and the ones who were joining us didn't come with the kind of training we'd had. Like the rest of the men who had gathered in England as June 6 approached, I had been well drilled and well trained over the course of many months. These new guys were a different story. Some of them had been civilians when our boys landed on Omaha Beach and Utah Beach. They'd been rushed through a brief version of basic training—the same training we'd spent seventeen weeks on—and then they were hurried from their homes to the front line of battle in the span of three months.

They weren't the only new soldiers we met. British and Canadian troops were fighting to liberate France as well, and it wasn't unusual for us to meet members of the French Resistance who had somehow survived the four years of German occupation. Most of them were small in stature, most likely due to the living conditions they'd endured under Hitler's men, but they fought like giants. We gave them whatever weapons we could spare and stood in awe when they took chances the rest of us would have shied away from.

Being a radio man suited me well, especially since the lieutenant I was assigned to was a Christian too—despite the fact that he was a Michigan man and I was from Ohio. I admired him for his single-mindedness and self-discipline. Even when chaos was swirling around him, he wouldn't allow himself to be distracted. Watching him reminded me of the lesson I'd learned in the skies above Washington State when I stalled my plane and killed the engine—that no matter what happens, you can never lose focus.

It was a lesson I tried to pass on to others as well. In the northern part of France one day, we came across some Germans who were hard to push back. We had lost so many men that there were only three of us in the squadron at the time, and it was all we could do to hold them and wait until we were replaced by another infantry outfit. We'd dug in near the top of a tree-lined knoll, and we stayed there most of the day. We exchanged fire from time to time, taking care to keep our heads below the top of the knoll and to avoid stepping in front of the five-foot gap in the trees.

Eventually the six new boys arrived. I didn't have to look at their boots or see them fight to know that they'd been in combat for only a few days—a week or two at most. Their eyes told their story more clearly than anything else. They had the look of fear in them, all right, but that wasn't exclusive to first-timers. What gave them away was the expression of shock. They had yet to come to terms— as much as any of us ever could—with the fact that this was war and there was no escaping it.

I told them that I didn't know how many Germans were on the other side of the slope but that they were in the tree line a hundred feet ahead of us. "And don't go near that break," I said, pointing to the gap in the trees. "They've got a machine gun trained on it."

The three of us from my squad backed down the hedgerow and prepared to make the half-mile trip back to our company. "God bless you," I said to the new guys as we all moved out.

"God?" one of the older-looking men spat out. "I don't need God. I can take care of myself."

I hoped he could. I turned back to take one last look

at the men and saw one of them take a step into the gap
I'd warned them about. Before I could shout a warning, a
burst of machine-gun fire sounded from the other side of
the knoll. I saw the soldier fall down, his head thrown back
at an impossible angle.

The Germans followed up with a short barrage of
mortar fire, but they fell short of their target. When the
sounds of the attack faded, all I could hear was my new
atheist friend sobbing into the earth. "Oh God!" he cried.
"Oh God! Help me!"

Almost every day we lost men. Some we lost because
they made mistakes; some we lost because the SS fought
desperately, savagely. Some we lost to our own weapons,
like the sergeant who died when we got strafed by our own
P-47s; and some we lost to the enemy's 88s and Screaming
Mimis—rockets full of oil and phosphorus that had a
range of several miles and could lift a man clean out of his
foxhole. The truth was, there were a hundred ways to die
out there and only one way to survive. You just had to find
the courage to keep going. That was the only way any of us
had a chance of survival.

Though I'd been a little timid on that first day of fighting back in Normandy, I'd grown braver over the course of
the summer. I still didn't enjoy using weapons, but at least
by then I'd been through enough battles and skirmishes
to trust myself to fight well. Even so, I have to admit I

was surprised when the chief called me in to give me some good news.

Back in Florida I'd been asked to stay behind at Camp Blanding to take on the rank of corporal, but it was a temporary assignment, and I'd given up the title as soon as I deployed. After Saint-Lô, I'd been promoted to corporal again, this time permanently. Now, just after we crossed from France into Belgium, the chief ordered me to report to him immediately.

"Corporal Whipps?" he said. "You're a staff sergeant now. You've sort of been leading the men anyway."

"Thank you, sir." I said. And I meant it. Being a staff sergeant wouldn't change the amount of time I'd spend fighting, and it wouldn't change the food I ate or give me a warmer coat to wear, but it would bring in a little more money and a lot more responsibility. For me, the money was irrelevant. I never saw mine; instead, I chose to have it paid into my account at home and not touch it while I was in France. The way I saw it, the Army gave me everything I needed to keep my body going. For everything else, I relied on God alone.

We were pushing the Germans back the way they'd come. Four years earlier, they'd bypassed the Maginot Line—the series of defense positions the French had built along their northeastern border—and invaded Luxembourg and Belgium before pouring south into France and smashing through weaker parts of the line. The Germans must have noted how easy it was for them to break through, because in the years leading up to our second front in Normandy, they'd been busy constructing a far stronger defensive line that stretched from Denmark in the north all the way to Italy in the south.

The Siegfried Line was a miles-wide band of impenetrable pillboxes (low bunkers for machine guns) with eleven-foot-thick walls and concrete antitank wedges that stuck out of the ground like a barbed-wire scar. It was miles long, and the only way to finish the war was to cross it.

Thoughts of the Siegfried Line troubled many of us as we fought our way across Luxembourg. With a squad of twelve men now under my command, I felt an extra burden settle onto my chest. It was one thing to figure out how I was going to get myself past the last line of German defenses, but it was another thing entirely to get my men safely through as well.

Though sergeants didn't get any extra rations, officers received a monthly allowance of liquor. It was my misfortune to serve under Lieutenant Boise, who drank more than he should have—to the point that it started to affect his judgment.

One day we were nearing a small town not far from the Siegfried Line.

"Sergeant Whipps," Lieutenant Boise said. "You see that house down there?" He was pointing at a small farmhouse that was flanked by two pillboxes. The house was down a hill, just a couple of hundred feet away.

"Yes, sir," I said. I could smell the liquor on his breath.

"I want you to take your squad down there and see if you can draw any fire."

Of all the ways to find out whether there were Germans in the pillbox or the farmhouse, this must have been the most foolish of them all. We could have waited until dark to make the approach, or we could have thrown in some of our mortars to flush them out. But Boise was set on sending me down without delay.

There was nothing I could do but say, "Yes, sir" and then go back to brief my men.

I had to hide my displeasure as I told them about the plan, but I wanted to prepare them as best I could. These were good men, though *men* might have been a stretch, as I doubted whether some of them had started shaving yet. Private Reeder was an Ohio man like me, with a heavy frame and a good-natured laugh. Private Goodwin was short and fast talking, a joker from Iowa whom I liked the moment I met him. Private First Class DeMaggio came from the East Coast and didn't talk much, but it usually wasn't hard to guess what those dark eyes of his were thinking as they peered out from beneath his helmet. They all listened carefully as I called them to gather around.

All the men in my squad had been deployed after the Saint-Lô breakthrough. They'd been fighting for only about a month, and so far their experience had consisted mainly of riding on tanks or fighting on a line with the twenty men who made up our platoon. They'd never been sent out like this before, never been put at this kind of risk. My mind flashed back to the day Tennessee died, but I closed my eyes to shake away the memory.

"We have to go down there and check out the house," I said. "We aren't going to get too close, but if they start firing at us, get back up this hill as fast as you can."

They looked as unsure as I felt, but we didn't see a way out. An order was an order, and there was no way we were going to disobey it.

As we checked our rifles and ammunition, I added one final instruction: "And if we have to run, don't get in my way."

The four of us moved down the hill, keeping a good distance between us so we didn't present a tempting target for any German snipers who might be watching us. Step by step we approached, each yard taking us farther from the safety of the hill and closer to whatever might be hiding there. I knew the Germans would wait until we were close before they opened fire, and each second that passed added another pound of pressure to the muscles in my chest. I had to concentrate hard to breathe, each inhalation threatening to crack open my lungs.

We must have been fifty feet from the farmhouse, not yet at the bottom of the hill, when a barn door flew open. I saw a flash of a German uniform in the space where the door had been and the glint of what looked like an anti-tank gun.

"Run!" I shouted as I turned back up the hill.

I sprinted up the hill, and immediately instinct and adrenaline took over. I could sense the other men with me, and I pinned my eyes on the top of the hill. "Run!"

I tried to shout again, but I had no breath to spare.

I heard the shell the instant it was fired—the familiar clank of metal on metal—then the sound of the air being ripped apart as the shell knifed toward us. Then, just a fraction of a second later, there was a heavy thud as it landed on the ground about eight feet to my right. I should have died at that moment. My whole squad should have died. But there was no explosion—none at all.

I didn't have time to stop and ponder the miracle. I knew that the Germans could fire again within seconds, and I doubted we'd be so lucky the next time.

I pressed on to the top. As I ran, it struck me that we'd come about as close to death as possible. I'd heard of dud shells before. I knew that many of the German artillery factories were staffed by female slave laborers who had been captured in Poland, France, and elsewhere and that when they could, they deliberately sabotaged the munitions.

I was filled with gratitude to the unknown factory girl, but that wasn't enough to dispel my anger. As soon as I'd cleared the brow of the hill and made sure my men had made it too, I walked straight up to Lieutenant Boise. He looked up from the map he was holding and caught my eye for a moment. His face was taut, his eyes anxiously flicking back to the map. I'd never gotten angry at an officer before—I'd been raised to show respect to those in authority. But right then, seconds after escaping death, I didn't feel relieved to be alive. I just felt enraged.

I had no idea why Boise had made such an impulsive choice and sent us down the hill, but I didn't care to find out. I just wanted him to know that his foolishness had nearly gotten four men killed.

"Don't ever do that again," I said.

He just looked at me. He could have disciplined me for talking to him like that, and for a moment I wondered if he was weighing his options. But then his eyes dropped to his hands, concentrating on folding the map he'd been examining.

I turned and walked away.

9

FACING THE LINE

I woke to the familiar smell of cold earth just inches from my face. Even in my drowsy state, I knew that this was the big day. As I did every morning, I silenced my breath and focused my attention on what I could hear. Nothing today, apart from Private Reeder's labored breathing next to me. I waited a second or two before pulling back the raincoat I used as a makeshift tarp.

It had been cold during the night. I thought about how Reeder had been griping about the lack of winter uniforms, and I wondered if he'd been able to sleep. I hoped so. I needed everyone in my squad to be ready for the day ahead.

The sky wasn't light yet—not fully, at least—but above

me I could see a streak of dark cloud curving up like a giant tail. The first splash of color was starting to light up one corner of the sky.

For the first time since landing in Normandy, I'd had a dream the night before. I couldn't remember the content, but I could still feel the residue of fear and tension within me, as if someone had poured a layer of thick mud over my uniform during the night. The last time I'd been able to get cleaned up was when we were outside Paris, and it hadn't taken my clothes long to regain their familiar odor and texture. Thankfully the smells of sweat, dirt, and filth had become so commonplace that they receded into the background by now. But the feel of cold, damp fabric against my skin was a constant irritation, like an itch that was impossible to scratch.

I waited as long as I could before checking my boots for lizards, putting them on, and getting out of my foxhole. I nudged my foxhole companion on the way.

"On your feet, Reeder." I said. "Let's go."

He grunted from under his raincoat.

Almost a week had passed since Lieutenant Boise had sent us down to the farmhouse. I hadn't gotten in any trouble for what I said to him afterward, and he acted as if both his order and my response had never happened. I wasn't able to forget about it, however.

It was the closest I'd come to being killed so far, but it wasn't my personal safety I was concerned about. That incident showed me that I was now responsible not just for my own life but also for the lives of others. It was up to me to keep my men safe, to protect them not just from enemy fire but also from mistakes made on our own side.

Breakfast was the usual K rations—a can of chopped ham and eggs, some biscuits, coffee, and a cereal bar. I joined Adams, a tech sergeant, who was eating behind a small pile of logs.

"Today's the day, Ray," he said. "You ready for the Siegfried Line?"

"About as ready as I'll ever be, I guess."

"After what happened with the shell, I reckon you're going to be fine. Someone's looking out for you."

I nodded. "That's what I believe."

The men knew about my faith, but most of them didn't see things the way I did. Lieutenant Michigan, as I called him, was one of the few, and I hadn't seen him since we left Paris the previous month.

Adams and I continued eating in silence for a while.

"What's the line like?" I asked.

"Big. The Germans weren't going to make the same mistake the French made with the Maginot Line, so they've made the Siegfried impossible to get around. We've got to go through it—that's the only way." He took another swig of his coffee. "There are pillboxes big enough to hold a hundred men, ack-ack guns all over the place, and antitank defenses."

By the time Adams and I had landed in France, all the pillboxes had been taken. But we knew what had happened at Omaha Beach—and how many of our men had been lost in the push to capture the German defenses. We'd heard that some of their pillboxes had concrete walls that were eleven feet thick and were so strong that everything our bombers dropped on them just bounced off. With the Germans firing through thin slits, the only way to take them was to lay down suppressing fire and send enough men forward. Not all of them would make it, but hopefully one would get close enough to be able to hurl a grenade inside.

"There's a guy back at company who landed at Omaha," Adams said. "He says the pillboxes are the toughest things he's faced so far. He claims that they're death traps. Our only hope is that we've got more men than they've got bullets."

This wasn't what I wanted to hear, but it was the truth. We were about to face our biggest challenge of the war so far, and the reality was that not all of us would make it. Instinctively, I felt for my Bible in my breast pocket.

"You know what I think?" Adams nodded at me. "I think if a bullet has my number on it, it'll get me."

We didn't have time to wait around, so I found my squad and made sure they were ready. "We're the first American troops at this point on the line," I told them. "But we're going to take it one pillbox at a time. It'll be just like before: run when I run; stop when I stop. Got it?"

They were too nervous to talk much, and I was feeling the same way. I looked up at the sky. Dawn had come, and thick, low clouds had swept in overhead.

I looked at the other men in the platoon as they got ready. Some of them were like Reeder, Goodwin, and DeMaggio, nervously preparing for their first taste of real combat. Others were even less experienced, still figuring out how to strap on their equipment right. Only a few of us were veterans on this squad. The rest of the faces were new, including some men who were returning from England, where they'd been recovering from wounds. These men had landed on Utah Beach, breaking through Hitler's Atlantic Wall. It seemed cruel to me that they'd been forced to return so soon.

We wore all our equipment strapped to our backs and waists: raincoat, shovel, K rations, medical kit, and water canteen. The packs had become so familiar to us that it felt odd when we took them off.

"Remember Joshua 1:9," I said to my boys as we prepared to walk the mile to the Siegfried Line. "Be strong and of good courage. Be not afraid and be not dismayed. The Lord is with thee."

It started to rain before we began walking, and even though most of our route took us through a thick forest, we were fairly wet by the time we approached the edge of the woods. We'd already been given our orders and we knew where to take our positions, so we peeled off, squad by squad, crouching low as we made our way toward the open space beyond the trees.

At last we reached the edge of a shallow valley that stretched down to our left and a little way up to our right. I looked ahead, and perhaps a quarter of a mile or so away, on the other side of the valley, I saw something that left me nearly paralyzed with fear. Running along the bare valley floor was a perfectly laid-out tank defense, made up of hundreds of concrete barriers that looked like waist-high pyramids. Every hundred feet or so, the line took a sharp turn left or right. There were dozens of these pillboxes throughout the valley, laid out to give a clear view of anyone approaching.

"This war's never going to end," Goodwin said.

I didn't agree with him. I couldn't. The idea of a war without end just didn't make any sense to me. What worried me more was the thought that gripped my chest like a metal brace: *How are we ever going to do anything here?*

It seemed to me that the Siegfried Line was impenetrable—a perfect German defense. As soon as we stepped out from the cover of the trees, we would be exposed. If the German machine guns, 88s, and Screaming Mimis didn't get us before we reached the line, we wouldn't have much chance of hiding behind these concrete dragons that stretched out before us. Even if we managed to hide, we'd have to avoid the German snipers as we tried to reach the pillboxes themselves. The only way I could see us making it would be with God's help.

"Remember, boys," I said as we waited quietly for the signal to go, "be strong and of good courage, and don't forget to do exactly as we said."

★

The silence before battle is like no other silence on earth. There is no peace in the stillness, no quiet moment when soldiers pause and collect themselves before the storm breaks. It's more like the start of a horse race, where the riders strain and pull and try to hold back their mounts. Of course, if anyone had seen us as we prepared to fight, they wouldn't have seen us moving or straining to go. On the outside we were quiet and still, but inside it was all we could do to keep in check the fear and adrenaline rearing up within us.

The rain was falling heavier now. I forced myself to concentrate on what was about to happen and ran through the plan again in my mind. I pictured myself sprinting, my feet moving swiftly and surely over the ground. I saw myself hiding behind the dragon's teeth (the concrete formations that prevented tanks from crossing). My body was curled up tight, invisible to the Germans in the pill-boxes beyond. And I saw myself running faster than ever to cover the ground between the teeth and pillboxes. And then, at last, I imagined arriving safely at the thick wall with all my men.

I knew that Goodwin, Reeder, and DeMaggio were beside me, but I didn't want to take my eyes off the scene in front of me to check. I trusted that they were there, waiting and watching. And I trusted that God was with me as well. *Grant me courage*, I prayed.

The first shots from our guns acted as a detonator that set my feet running. I locked my eyes on the concrete pyramid ahead that looked bigger than the rest and shouted, "Let's go!"

We all took off, and I did my best to ignore the sound of gunfire filling the air. All I needed was speed.

I reached the dragon's teeth quickly, but not the tall one I'd aimed for. Somehow I'd veered a little to the left as I ran. I was annoyed with myself for making a mistake like that—I should have been more focused. Keeping myself as small as I could, I looked up. I saw the rest of my squad, along with the others, up and down the line. I looked back at the trees we'd just run from. Where it had been clear before, there were now a handful of men down on the ground.

I pulled my gaze back to the pillbox we'd been assigned. It was close, not much farther than thirty or forty feet away. I doubted that it was big enough to hold more than a dozen soldiers—not that it made much difference, because out of the single slit of a window, I saw the familiar dark gray of a German machine gun, spitting out fire and bullets. Whether there was one man inside or ten, the gun ensured that the odds were stacked against us.

My ears were exploding with the sounds of gunfire all around me. There was the clap of bullets as they whipped by, the splinter as they hit the concrete around us, and the whoosh and crush of mortars as they tore up the ground. Underneath the noise of weapons, I could hear men calling out from both sides.

"Watch the line!"

"Suppressing fire!"

"Let's go! Let's go!"

I'd been firing at our pillbox ever since I'd spotted the machine gun through the slit. Whether I'd hit anyone or not I couldn't tell, but I finished the round in my rifle, reloaded, and looked at my squad. "Come on," I said to Goodwin. "Let's go."

Just as we'd planned, Reeder and DeMaggio concentrated their fire on the pillbox, sending a continual storm of bullets into the opening. Keeping low and gripping my rifle tightly in front of me, I took a deep breath. Then I moved out from behind the concrete and ran forward. Within three or four strides, I was clear of the dragon's teeth. It was only about ten more steps to the pillbox, but it felt like ten miles. With every step I kept my eyes on the pillbox, willing Reeder and DeMaggio to keep up their attack and the German guns to remain out of sight.

Just before I reached the front of the pillbox, I lost my footing. Thankfully, however, I had enough momentum to carry me, scrambling, over the ground to the wall. The slit was low, and I had to work hard to keep myself down far enough to remain out of sight. I pressed my back against the concrete. I could feel its rough finish through my uniform. Goodwin pulled up beside me, breathing heavily. We each grabbed a grenade, nodded at each other, and pulled out the big metal pins that stuck out from the sides. One, two, three. Throw.

We ducked. I didn't feel anything through the wall, just the same rough concrete against my back. Yet through the window slit came a blast of air, dust, debris, and noise.

I looked up to see the others running toward us. We all moved to the back of the pillbox and waited while Reeder looked in.

"It's clear," he said.

It was almost impossible to tell how long the maneuver had taken. It felt as though days had passed since we'd run out from the trees, but I knew it was probably only a couple of minutes.

"Good work," I panted as we crouched down in the doorway.

From our new vantage point, we could see a little farther up the valley. There were no more antitank defenses ahead, but there were plenty of pillboxes. Everything we'd done so far was just the beginning.

The rest of the day we carried on the same way. We fought our way up the other side of the valley, taking more pillboxes. Some were empty, the Germans having fled before we reached them, but others seemed to take hours to win.

As daylight began to fade, we joined up with another squad and decided to concentrate our fire on the biggest pillbox we'd seen that day. It was the size of a house, surrounded by thick trees. It looked impenetrable, but all we could do was trust that the same tactics we'd been using would continue to work. We concentrated our fire on the openings, our bullets raining down like a Midwestern hailstorm.

That was when the sound roared above us. I'd heard the noise before, and I knew to hit the ground hard.

I counted four rockets passing by, not far overhead. I guessed they must have been aiming at our artillery farther back, but that thought didn't do much to calm me. And based on the looks on the faces around me, I could tell everyone else was as terrified as I was.

★

Later that night, dug into a foxhole, I thought about the day. I replayed again the sound of the Screaming Mimis and hoped never to hear them again. It was a childish wish, but I clung to it all the same. I replayed the rain and the feel of the wet grass on my face while diving for cover. I remembered the smells of ammunition that stained the air and still hung heavy on my clothes. I thought of Goodwin, Reeder, and DeMaggio and thanked God that they had survived this day.

I tried not to remember the dead men I'd seen. Germans and Americans—my mind offered me both. I'd seen our own men cut up by German bullets and shrapnel, and I'd seen Germans killed by our bullets and grenades. I forced the images out of my mind. They would do me no good.

I chose instead to remember a conversation that Adams and I had as we walked out that morning.

"You know what's beyond all this, don't you?" he'd asked me.

"Beyond the line?" I asked. "No, I don't."

"There's a forest. The Krauts have been in there for months, preparing their defenses. The Siegfried Line is a picnic by comparison."

My mouth was dry, and I could barely swallow. Even as I tasted fear, I knew there was only one way we were going to make it through.

"Well," I said, "I guess we're all going to need Someone up there looking out for us."

It was strange, but somehow the nerves and the tension I'd felt earlier were gone. I was tired and ready for sleep, but underneath my fatigue was a sense of peace. God had been there. If not for Him, I wouldn't have survived the day. Knowing that I was helpless and dependent on Him wasn't such a bad thing after all.

I pulled the raincoat closer to me and listened as Reeder's breathing slowed. Tomorrow would be more of the same: more danger, more fear, and more need for God. I had no doubt that He would be there. No doubt at all.

167th General Hospital
Cherbourg, France

November 23, 1944

Dear Mom and Dad,

It's strange to be celebrating Thanksgiving here, eating in our canvas tent and preparing to work a twelve-hour shift that will start in just a couple of hours. We are such a long way from home, and the presence of turkey and all the trimmings can't lessen the distance between us, but it helps to be reminded of all that is good in life today. I am thankful for you—for your love, your kindness, your prayers. And I am thankful to God for bringing me here and for keeping me safe.

I am also thankful for these soldiers. So many of them have experienced such pain, some with terrible wounds caused by shrapnel that has carved through their flesh. Yet despite their cries and their knowledge that they will soon be sent back out to fight again, they display a level of courage I would never have thought possible.

Life has settled into a routine for me here, and I try to use my twelve hours off as wisely as possible. That means getting a little sleep, heating and eating my K rations, reading and writing letters, and spending time with the other nurses. After a week of night shifts, we swap to day shifts, and though it sounds tiring, we are all amazed how much energy we have. We are all still healthy, and I know I have your prayers and God's help to thank for that.

In many ways, the war feels a long way off. By the time the soldiers reach us, they have traveled a long way from the front and they are clearly relieved to be safe. But there is never a day that goes by without my being reminded just how much this all matters. I only have to look at these men to be reminded of that. They are offering their lives, and serving them is the least I can do.

Your loving daughter,
Betty

P.S. I still haven't figured out why they told us we needed a hammer here. Maybe it was just one of those Army things to make sure you can follow orders!

10

A NEW WAY OF FIGHTING

I'D NEVER SEEN MEN LOOKING so tired and broken. We were waiting back at battalion headquarters when they passed us—a long line of faces that were as worn as the uniforms that hung from their bodies. I couldn't take my eyes off them.

As they shuffled by, the noise of their boots sloshing through the wet mud was the only sound. The soldiers' red insignia marked them as men of the Twenty-Eighth Infantry, but they looked nothing like the courageous heroes they were reputed to be. Rumor had it that the Twenty-Eighth unit was made up of tough combatants who, like General Patton, fought hard and moved fast.

"Hard to believe they were the ones given the honor of marching through the Champs-Élysées a couple of months ago," said a voice in the watching crowd.

Though part of me wanted to, I couldn't look away from these men. I knew why the sight struck fear into me: we were their replacements. Where they had just come from, we were going.

When the last of their number had finally drifted past, I looked up at the sky. It was still heavy, streaked with the threat of rain. The air was colder, and it was obvious that winter was on the way, but the sky hadn't changed a bit. It seemed it had remained this shade of gray since we started our attack on the Siegfried Line.

For weeks we'd fought our way through the mud, crossing open fields and woodland glades along the border between Belgium and Germany. We'd taken pillbox after pillbox, sometimes fighting men as they stumbled out, other times feeling a sense of relief upon discovering that the posts had been abandoned before we arrived. Once we even found a stash of sardines that a squad had left behind. That was a good day.

We had lost men throughout the Twenty-Second, though my entire squad had made it through the fighting okay. I was grateful and relieved that Reeder, Goodwin, and DeMaggio were still with me. When the battle for the line was declared over, a few of the men who'd been serving for a while had been given a few days off and told to go enjoy the delights of Paris. Not me, though. Still, I was grateful that the fighting had calmed enough for me to recover a little. I rested up, read my Bible, and let myself soak in the relative peace and quiet of life away from the line. Some of the men complained of being bored, but I was happy just to be able to breathe again.

We all knew that we were pushing the Germans back week by week, and it felt good to be making progress. The psychological impact of forcing our way across their own border was significant, and some of our earlier optimism about being close to the war's end returned. Some, but not all. Ahead of us lay the Ruhr Valley and the Rhine River, plus the city of Cologne, and each of these spots was strategically significant. But before we could think about these challenges, we had to deal with the Hürtgen Forest. The Germans weren't going to let us through easily.

All of this was churning in our minds as we waited on the outskirts of the forest on November 6, 1944. We were aware that other divisions had gone into the forest and hadn't been able to get it under control, but it was only as we stood watching the men of the Twenty-Eighth that the scale of the task ahead of us became clear. If the Twenty-Eighth was in retreat, what kind of success could we hope for?

"The problem is the terrain," our commanding officer said as we watched them walk by. "It's hilly and covered in mud, and the trees are packed together so close that we can't get the tanks in. We're going up against defenses that the Krauts have been preparing for months. They've got machine-gun nests on the ground and snipers up in the trees. They've laid mines, and they're sending in their artillery so it will burst in the trees and then send out splinters along with the shrapnel. They know exactly where we are. We don't."

Silently, I turned over the words of the Bible that had given me so much comfort in the five months since landing in France. Only this time, as we stepped onto the muddy path that led us away from the battalion and up to the line, it felt harder than ever to be strong. Could I really conquer my fear when every exhalation brought with it the temptation to scream out loud?

Even though the marching drills had seemed alien and almost unnecessary back home, there had already been so many times when I'd been grateful for the training I received. This was one of them. Having watched the Twenty-Eighth shuffle out, knowing that they were the lucky ones, the survivors, my civilian instincts would have told me to flee. But I was a soldier, and I knew I had a simple job to do. I had to follow orders, just like every other man around me. And at that moment, as the clouds grew even heavier and I shivered inside my wool uniform, my job was to move up to the line.

Lord, I prayed, my heart racing, *give me courage. Let me know that You are with me.*

Step by step, in sync with the pair of boots ahead of me, I walked forward. It was all I could do. Thankfully, it was all I had to do.

I don't remember how long it took us to walk to the forest itself. It was probably a matter of minutes, but in my memory there was something endless about the journey. I kept my eyes fixed on the soldier in front of me. There was no need to look ahead to see how close we were to our destination, just as there was no need to look behind me to see a trail of men just like me, moving forward one step at a time.

When I finally looked up, it was because the sky had grown even darker. We'd made it to the edge of the forest, and the towering fir trees were blocking out the little light we had. The trees were packed so tightly together that I couldn't see much more than eighty feet ahead. But there was no mistaking the sounds coming from inside the forest. The gunfire and artillery were far enough away for now, but these were the sounds of war, all right.

Once we'd been given our instructions, we moved up to the line. We were replacements, hand delivered to fill positions that another unit had fought for. Just like the men from the Twenty-Eighth I'd been staring at earlier, the soldiers we moved past looked beyond exhausted. There was no time to stand and gawk, however. A handful of other soldiers and I were immediately sent out to investigate a new possible place of attack.

My first impressions of the forest—how dark it was, with limited visibility—were almost right. But eighty feet was a wildly optimistic figure—I realized I'd be lucky to be able to see twenty or thirty feet ahead. And there was something eerie about the light in there. It wasn't just dark; it was gray, as if all the color had been washed out of the world.

We moved forward slowly, spread out among the trees. Looking up, I could see the aftermath of artillery shells that had detonated twenty feet overhead. It was as if some giant hand had reached down and grabbed every tenth tree, pulling violently and shredding its branches. All around us, the forest floor was covered with a carpet of mud and splintered wood.

The first clap of a bullet took me by surprise. I threw myself down, near one of the larger logs that lay discarded on the ground. Another shot came in, and I pressed myself tighter against the wood.

I glanced up when I saw another man from the Twenty-Second join me behind the log. I didn't remember seeing him before.

"Sniper," I whispered. "Did you see him?"

He nodded just as another bullet came in. This one was closer, hitting somewhere in front of our log. Immediately the air was filled with the sound of someone moaning in agony. Judging by the sound, the wounded man was just on the other side of the log. Without even conferring about it, the other soldier and I jumped up, reached over the log, and grabbed a handful of the man's uniform. A bullet whizzed by our heads, ripping the air as it went. But

I managed to get one hand on his jacket and another on his arm, and we hauled him over before the sniper got any more shots off.

When I got a look at the man's face, I saw that it was our first-aid man. He was in a bad way. He'd been shot in the lower part of his chest, and the blood was coming out fast. Another bullet came in above us, this time so close it almost skimmed my helmet. I pressed farther down into the ground.

To my right, I saw one of our men move out side-ways from behind the log that was giving him cover. He aimed his rifle high into the trees and fired off two shots. The silence that followed was both welcome and disturb-ing. Had he gotten the sniper, or was the German simply keeping quiet until we came out from our cover?

"Clear!" came the shout, and my body relaxed just a little.

"Gimme a shot," the first-aid man said as we tried to stop the bleeding.

I'd never given anyone morphine before, and I wasn't sure how to do it. Judging by the look in the other soldier's eyes, neither was he. I looked around, not sure where to look for the medical supplies.

"I don't know how to do this," I told the first-aid man. "Tell me what to do."

His eyes were squeezed shut, and the pain must have been unbearable. He was desperate, but he wasn't able to utter anything other than "Morphine!"

I considered looking through his kit in an attempt to

find the right vial and administer it, but I knew I was in over my head. I turned my head in the direction we'd come and yelled, "Medic!"

It didn't take long before a medic arrived. His hands moved quickly as he poured a small packet of white powdered sulfur over the wound to prevent infection and administered morphine for the pain.

There was nothing else for us to do, and with the sniper dead, we moved out from behind the safety of the log. My rifle stuck to my hands where the blood acted like a weak glue, but there was no time to stop and clean up. If there had been one sniper around here, it stood to reason that there could be more, and I didn't want to be a sitting target again.

The next day and the one after that, we were introduced to a new way of fighting. In some ways it was similar to the fighting we'd done at the Siegfried Line or during our advances in hedgerow country. For one thing, our advances were measured in yards rather than miles as we'd done when riding with General Patton. And we still relied on good men to know what to do without being told, just as we always had. But in one vital way Hürtgen Forest was unlike any other fighting we'd experienced up to this point: its sheer intensity.

Here among the shattered trees and suffocated daylight, there was no breakfast-time silence, no lull while both sides ate in what passed for peace. The fighting was nearly constant, and when there was a pause, more often than not we were the ones who broke it. I pictured the Germans happily dug into foxholes or taking refuge behind thick-walled pillboxes while dogfaces like me were trying to survive out on the forest floor.

It was as if we were in a never-ending race. Whenever there was time enough to eat, we did so quickly and silently, never lollygagging or taking time to talk. When there was a lull, all we could think about was how long we'd have to wait until the fighting resumed. And when the air was filled with shells and splinters, we'd wonder how long it would be until the barrage ceased. We learned how to remove our helmets and use our rifles to raise them just high enough above the top of a foxhole to draw German fire. If none came, it was safe enough to move out of the foxhole. At least, we hoped it was.

The Germans had us so well pinned down that our progress was painfully slow. Sometimes we'd fight all day and advance only by three or four trees. We'd have to dig new foxholes and try our best to cover them with logs to protect us from the splinters and shrapnel that inevitably rained down on us. It was hard fighting, and bit by bit the pressure was starting to show.

A few days after we arrived, there was a break in the weather. The rain eased up, and for the first time one morning, I glimpsed something other than heavy, gray clouds beyond the charred treetops. No sunshine could make its way down to us on the forest floor, and the soldier I was sharing the foxhole with didn't want to talk much, but even so, it was good to be able to eat a tin of food without having to hide underneath a raincoat.

In an instant, everything changed. German artillery screamed into the space above our heads as explosion after explosion split the trees. It was deafening, so loud that it blocked out all other sounds. It was as if the very air itself were a minefield. All I could do—all any of us could do— was dive down and get as much cover as possible beneath a nearby log. I didn't dare to look up; I just sat with my eyes scrunched tight, my body curled into a ball, and prayed that God would end it soon.

In France the Germans might have thrown a few of their 88s, which would send us diving for cover if we guessed they were coming in close enough, but this warfare made everything else we'd experienced seem like child's play. The artillery was flying in and exploding twenty feet overhead, and the effects were devastating. Since none of the force of the blast was absorbed by the earth, the airbursts sent out chaos in all directions. Every hunk of timber within the radius of the shells' blasts was turned into deadly shrapnel, but instead of tiny shards of metal, it came in the form of bullet-size splinters.

I let myself peer out from under my helmet through a gap in the log above me. All I could see was a haze of flying timber. I couldn't imagine how anyone would survive this if they hadn't been hiding in a foxhole from the very start.

The explosions went on like this for minutes. Then, as quickly as it had started, the artillery attack faded. But while the crushing sound of artillery had vanished, in its place came other sounds—almost as terrifying. There was the noise of sporadic gunfire, from our side as well as theirs, but it was the sound of one man shouting from somewhere nearby that stood out most.

"Medic!" he cried. But his voice didn't have the same urgency that had filled my own voice when I'd called for someone to help the first-aid man. This wasn't the sound of someone who believed he could survive if only he got the right assistance. This was the sound of total panic, the sound of a helpless victim tortured by fear. It was the sound of a man waking from a nightmare and realizing it was only just beginning.

His screams carried on. I tried my best to fire back at the enemy, but in truth, I had no idea where I should have been firing. For the first time, I noticed the other soldier in my foxhole. He sat as I'd been sitting, back to the earth, knees hunched close to his body. But his helmet had fallen off, and his face was perfectly blank. He was staring—at what, I couldn't tell—and though I tried to get him to find his helmet, he just kept looking out at nothing. There was no getting through to him.

Between the screams of terror and the sight of a frozen comrade next to me, I was at a loss about what to do. Instinct kicked in, and I could do only two things: try to keep firing and cry out to God for help.

Just as my rifle sent bullets in the vague direction of the enemy, so my prayers were a jumbled mass of silent words and desperate longings. *Father God*, I prayed, *Father God.*

At last, the fighting slowed. The fear that had gripped my foxhole buddy slowly thawed, and the man who had been screaming was helped back down the line. It turned out that he wasn't even injured, just terrified by the sight of another man in his foxhole who had taken the full force of a blast.

Ten days or so passed as we engaged in this forest-style warfare, and then things started to get worse. It began with the weather. The temperature dipped so low one night that it was impossible to sleep for more than a few minutes. Our winter uniforms still hadn't arrived, and though we didn't lack firewood, it would have been suicide to light even the smallest fire in our foxholes. So we simply made ourselves as small as we could and burrowed into the ground.

One morning we woke to find snow all around us. The white blanket made the charred, splintered trees stand out even more. The cold was not our friend for many reasons, not the least of which was that whenever we managed to advance our position, we were faced with the added diffi-culty of digging new foxholes in frozen earth. Most fright-ening of all, some of the men were losing their instinct for self-preservation. They would kneel in half-dug holes and just stop digging.

Other soldiers took matters into their own hands. I heard of more than one man who shot himself in the foot. Some even paused midway through a battle, removed one boot and sock, and waved a foot just above the ridge of their foxhole, just as we did with our helmets. They figured that losing a toe was a small price to pay to get sent home. I wasn't so sure myself. Maybe I could survive without a toe, but how could I hope to live with the guilt and dishonor that took its place?

We started to talk among ourselves about the way things were going. It seemed as though we were getting drawn deeper and deeper into a battle that was costing us far too many men.

"I don't know what they're thinking," I said one evening after I'd climbed down into my foxhole. It wasn't like me to question the orders I'd received, but I wasn't sure how long my men could survive this.

"We could have isolated this area," the sergeant I was with said. "We could have just gone around. Eventually they'd run out of ammunition and food, and that would be that. But that isn't what the general wanted."

"You know what bothers me most?" I asked. "In the two weeks we've been here, I've only seen one German. They're too well dug in. Surely the general knew that before he sent us in."

Despite the fact that it was an Army tradition, griping never really seemed to help all that much. I still felt just as cold and just as unsafe.

11

ALONE

On my fourteenth day in the Hürtgen Forest, I awoke
to a morning that was just as cold, but at least it was dry. The
lack of new snow seemed to lift our spirits somewhat, and
we fought well all day. We advanced beyond a machine-gun
nest that we'd been concentrating on the day before, and we
pushed the Germans back farther than we had at any other
point in the battle. By the time the sky started to darken
and evening came, we were tired but happy to have survived
another day.

I liked to check on the men in my squad before I climbed
into my own foxhole each night, and I was moving as
quickly as I could between them.

"You fought well today," I told them. "Get some rest."

I don't know if the Germans had a spotter who could see me as I moved from foxhole to foxhole, but as I returned to my own spot in the ground, I heard the familiar sound of an 88 gun firing from the enemy line. I was only two or three paces away from safety, but I wasn't going to make it in time.

The shell landed a short distance behind me, sending a shock wave that threw me onto my back. The noise was still ringing in my ears when I realized I'd been hit. I put my hand to my right leg, and instead of the familiar feel of my rough wool uniform, my fingers met torn fabric and fragments of metal, all covered with something warm and sticky. I forced myself to look.

It was not a good sight. The uniform across my entire right thigh was shredded, and from beneath I could see a mash of blood and torn flesh.

The pain was similar to what I'd felt when my hands had been wounded, only this time it was much worse. The pain seemed to be coursing through my whole body, and for a moment it was all I could do to breathe and tell myself, *At least you're still alive.*

Tech Sergeant Anders, the head of the platoon, called out to ask if everyone was okay.

"No!" I shouted. "It's Whipps. I've been hit."

I looked at my body again, trying to assess the damage. Spanning the length of my thigh was a wide, jagged cut. It was hard to tell with all the blood, but it looked like it went several inches deep. I tried to sit up and rest my back against the trunk of a nearby tree. Every move made my leg burn white hot with pain.

Anders slid down beside me, looking at my leg before taking in the rest of my injuries. "Oh, Whipps," he said, ripping open a pack of sulfur and sprinkling it on my leg. "You're going to have to get out of here the best you can."

He filled my canteen with water and tied a bandage tight around my thigh. "Make sure you drink a lot, and go straight back to the aid station, okay?"

I was shaken, but the pain wasn't bad enough to make me pass out. *That's good,* I told myself. *I'm not going to die from a wound like this.*

Then again, I was bleeding pretty profusely, and if I didn't get to safety quickly, I might be in trouble. I let Anders help me up.

"I can make it," I said. The words sounded more confident out loud than they did in my head.

I set aside my rations, ammunition, and everything but my rifle and my pack, and then I leaned heavily on Anders. He took me about twenty feet behind the line.

"Don't forget to keep drinking." He patted me on the shoulder and then disappeared to his foxhole.

I stood still for a moment, thinking how quickly everything had changed. Not five minutes earlier, I'd been scurrying from foxhole to foxhole, checking on the men and thinking about how good it would feel to fall asleep. Now I was barely able to walk. Adrenaline had washed all traces of fatigue from my body, and the savage pain was enough to ensure that I wouldn't be thinking about sleep anytime soon. I looked at my leg and saw that patches of red were already starting to soak through. I wondered if the bandage would hold until I got back to the aid station.

I inhaled deeply and set off, using my rifle as a walking stick. Even with a makeshift crutch, there was no way to avoid putting pressure on my leg. Every time the injured leg hit the ground, another spasm of pain shot through me. *Just walk,* I told myself. *Take the next step. Good. Now take another. Okay.*

It was slow progress, and painful, but I took it one step at a time, one tree at a time. I recognized almost every one of the trees I passed, and even though I was hobbling at a snail's pace, I was moving back much faster than we'd advanced. Every few minutes I found myself at the site of a previous day's battle.

I must have gotten lost in my thoughts, because the sound startled me when I first heard it. I stopped and listened again. It was a man groaning, saying something I couldn't quite make out. I took a couple of steps closer to where the sound seemed to be coming from—a foxhole nearby.

"Help!" The voice was weak, barely audible. I took another step closer, to the edge of the foxhole, and peered in.

It was a German soldier. He was lying on his back, his legs and torso lifeless. It was almost dark, but I could see the thick streaks of blood on his face. They had dried to the color of mud.

"Help!" he said again. The strain of calling out must have been great, because he started to gag, causing fresh blood to leak out of his mouth.

I had to turn away. It wasn't too hard to do so; he was my enemy, and this was still war. Besides, I knew there was nothing I could do to help him—I had no medical supplies that could save him, and I was in no condition to try to carry him back to our aid station. I'd also heard about wounded German soldiers turning themselves into human booby traps using grenades. I had no desire to die that way.

I hurried off as best I could, and as I did, I realized that for the first time since landing in France, I was alone. For the past five months, I'd never been more than ten or twenty feet from another soldier. During the day I'd fought or waited alongside the others in my squad, and at night I'd shared a foxhole or a field with someone. But now there was nobody. It was just me, and I didn't like it.

I wondered whether I would make it. Would I get lost? Would my leg hold out? Would I meet another German, one I couldn't defend myself against?

I pressed on, trying to put these questions out of my mind. I needed courage, as I always did, but I needed comfort, too.

That's when the words of a song I'd sung as a child at church came into my mind.

Jesus loves me! This I know,
For the Bible tells me so;
Little ones to Him belong;
They are weak, but He is strong.

I sang those words over and over. On my lips, the song was quiet and tuneless as I struggled for breath and tried to swallow the pain. But in my head, the words were accompanied by a glorious choir.

Jesus loves me! He will stay
Close beside me all the way;
Thou hast bled and died for me;
I will henceforth live for Thee.

Though each step was still agony, I took comfort from those words. I was weak, but He was strong. He was close beside me all the way. And He Himself knew all about bleeding.

It was completely dark by the time I arrived at the aid station. A medic laid me down on a stretcher and carefully peeled off the bandage Anders had tied around me. As he lifted it off, I saw that it was soaked through. Hardly a single patch of white was visible.

"Whoever got to you first did a good job," he said. "Still, we're going to send you back as fast as we can, Sergeant. You'll most likely end up in Paris, but you'll go to Brussels first."

"And after Paris?" I asked.

"Maybe they'll send you somewhere else in Europe, or maybe you'll go to England. Either way, you're not bad enough to go to the States."

"That's good," I said.

"Good? How so?"

"If I'm not going home, it means I'm not too badly injured."

The next morning, just as the sun rose, I was loaded onto an ambulance that took me and a couple of other wounded men to Brussels. We arrived at the two-story brick hospital just as they were serving dinner. They were serving the typical K rations, but they'd been transformed into a feast by being heated.

By the time they brought my supper, I was dressed in fresh pajamas and delighting in the comfort of lying on a proper cot. It had been twenty-four hours since I'd left the Hürtgen Forest and five months since I'd slept on anything other than the ground. I couldn't remember the last time I'd worn pajamas. My body almost didn't know what to do with such luxury.

The next day I sat on my bed, read my Bible, and just stared into space. I barely noticed the other men around me, but when I did look around the room, I saw that almost every other person was engaged in the same activities: sleeping, staring, or reading. Nobody else had a Bible out, but I was used to that by now.

The afternoon stretched out before me, and I was dozing when one of the nurses ran into the room.

"Bomb!" she shouted.

Immediately I heard a vaguely familiar but terrifying sound. The slow, steady pulse of an engine was growing louder, the whirring noise coming closer and closer. Even if I hadn't been injured, I'm not sure I would have been able to climb off my bed. The noise pinned me down. I was helpless.

I'd heard buzz bombs—or V-1s, as the Germans called them—before. They were simple but devastating, and they had the hallmark German quality of sounding terrifying. They were powerful, too, and when this one hit the building, all the windows smashed in an instant. I felt my leg explode in pain again, and I looked down to see my white bandages slowly turning pink, then red.

It took less than twelve hours to get enough of us together to fill an ambulance and take us from Brussels to Paris. When we arrived at the hospital there, it was obvious from the number of men and the lack of doctors that this was just another location where they would assess us and then send us somewhere else.

"It's going to take time for that to heal," a doctor told me. "So you'll go back to England."

Being out of the range of buzz bombs seemed like good news to me.

"You'll fly out tomorrow."

Only by the time the next day came, the plans had changed again. A heavy winter's fog had settled over the city, and I was told that no planes would be flying out that day.

I received my new set of marching orders: "You'll be staying in France. We're putting you on the train to Cherbourg."

The last time I'd been in Cherbourg was when it was the scene of fierce fighting, but I knew all that must have changed by now. So I did what I'd done all along in the war: I followed orders and kept waiting.

The train was full of men like me, many of them looking anxious as we pulled out of the train station. By the time the fog lifted, we'd left the city far behind. From the window, I could see nothing but trees and flat fields. With every field and every town we passed, I felt myself relax a little more.

"Sergeant Whipps?" Hearing my name pulled me out of my daydreaming. "Sergeant Whipps, is that you?" I looked up to see a young man looking at me from the other side of the train.

I recognized him, but like me, he was out of his uniform and wearing pajamas. Eventually I placed him. He was a young private who had been in my platoon—one of the replacements. His shoulder was heavily bandaged.

"I heard you were wounded," he said as he came to stand by the bench where I was lying. "What happened?"

I told him about being out of my foxhole and the single 88 that had come in. I said that Anders had bandaged me up well and that I'd been able to make it safely to the aid station. I didn't say anything about the German soldier, though. I didn't know how I would have told that story even if I'd wanted to.

"What about you?" I asked. "What happened after I left?"

He looked straight at me. "Your squad was wiped out. The day after you left, the Krauts hit your boys hard. There was nothing they could do but stay in their foxholes and wait until it was over."

It was too much to take in. Part of me felt relieved and grateful that I'd been pulled out of the Hürtgen Forest before the attack, but another part couldn't fathom why I'd survived when the others had not.

The private told me a little more about the attack—how some had been killed and some had been so badly injured that they were taken away from the line to be treated. I could hardly absorb what he was saying. What I kept thinking about was that if I'd been there with my squad that day, I would have been under that same attack. No doubt those who had survived sustained injuries far worse than mine.

So where was God in all this? Had He used my injury to get me away from the front line? If so, why would He do that?

Eventually the private and I reached the end of our conversation, and he returned to the other side of the train car. I tried to make sense of the thoughts that crowded in my mind, but I couldn't. I stared out the window, watching town after town and field after field roll by. As the train's rhythm filled my ears, the words of the song returned to me.

Jesus loves me still today,
Walking with me on my way,
Wanting as a friend to give,
Light and love to all who live.

A part of me wanted to sing the words out loud—to give them air to make them true. I wanted "light and love to all who live," but I couldn't get the words out. I didn't have the strength within me to do it.

12

SHRAPNEL OF THE HEART

It was dark when I opened my eyes. At first I wondered whether it was the pain in my leg that had woken me, but the dream returned with each gulp of air I took. Soon I remembered it clearly. I was wounded, lying on the ground in the Hürtgen Forest. I'd pulled myself up and was sitting with my back against the tree. My leg was bloodied and torn up, just as it had been in real life, only this time I could see all the way to the bone. In front of me the men of my squad were dug safely into their foxholes, shivering in pairs and eating cold K rations.

I couldn't see the men's faces in my dream, but I knew exactly who they were: my men, my squad. They made me proud. Yet almost as soon as this feeling registered within me, I began to feel anxious. I was stuck, immobile, as if both my legs had been shot off entirely. While their foxholes had appeared safe at first, I now saw that they were traps—like something a hunter might lay for his prey.

I tried to shout and urge the men to move, but no sound came out of my mouth. Instead, my dream was filled with the noise I'd heard in the hospital in Brussels— the gnawing, droning sound that belonged to a V-1 bomb. The noise grew louder and louder in my dream until my whole chest began to shake. But still my men sat hunched in their foxholes, unaware of the danger closing in on them.

I tried to shout again, to push myself up and run toward them, but my mouth and my body refused to work. Just when I thought the sound couldn't get any louder, it stopped. Silence settled around me. But it didn't last. Suddenly there was a noise like the tearing of a thousand trees from their roots. Splinters and flames started swirling together in terrifying clouds of smoke and earth.

As the chaos grew more intense, I tried to change the direction of the dream, but I had no power. I knew I didn't want to see inside the foxholes, and I strained to look away, but it was no use. My gaze fell on each one. Against my will, I saw twisted bodies, flesh turned inside out, blood mixed with mud, fabric, and metal.

At last my breathing slowed, and the dream faded into the background. I looked around the makeshift hospital room, hoping to distract myself from the images burning behind my eyelids. The darkness was softening a bit, and my eyes began to pick out shapes that filled the tent. I was in the last of a long row of beds that stretched off to my left. Beyond my cot were others just like it, and to my side was the canvas of the tent. It was cold, all right, and even though I could see the soft glow of amber light coming from the potbellied stove near the foot of my bed, I couldn't feel its warmth.

I remembered little of the tent from when I'd been brought in late the previous evening. I remembered being cold, but I was beyond caring about much by that point. The two days I'd spent being transported from place to place had drained me of what little energy I had left. I hadn't said much since the nurse told me I should get some sleep and that I would be seen by a doctor in the morning. Yet as much as my body wanted to do exactly that, my thoughts kept me awake. The news that my squad had been wiped out—many of them dead, others injured badly enough to be withdrawn from combat— plagued me. No wonder my living nightmare had taken over my dreams.

Apart from the usual sounds you'd expect to hear in a tent full of men—the varying grunts and snorts of air going in and air going out—it was quiet. I guessed that it was early, but I wanted to know what time it was. I remembered the nurse telling me that she'd placed the few possessions I'd brought with me in a box underneath my bed. I swung down my arm and groped around for a while before I found it. There wasn't much inside, and I quickly found my watch. I knew it would be too dark to see it, but holding it made me feel better.

I felt inside the box again. There was my Bible. It was good to be able to hold it and feel the soft curl of the page corners, even if it was too dark to read. I felt around some more. There was the familiar shape of my letters from home, the photograph that showed my parents standing outside our house on East Maynard Avenue. I'd looked at these keepsakes so many times that it didn't matter how dark it was. I could see them just as well in my mind.

Then I came to one item that was less familiar. It was smooth and circular, and it took a moment before I realized what it was. It was a simple gold ring. My mind rewound to the afternoon when I'd taken it from a German soldier. It was a week, maybe two, before we'd moved up to the Siegfried Line. We'd been fighting around a small village outside Houffalize, and a squad of Germans had given themselves up when they saw we had them surrounded. They shuffled in front of the house they'd been hiding behind and meekly held up their hands in surrender.

The soldiers looked old and tired, just like their uniforms. They weren't SS, just regular infantrymen who had likely been forced to put on German uniforms and fight for a leader they hadn't chosen. I let someone else deal with them and walked around the corner to where they'd been fighting. One of their number was lying on the ground—alive, but only barely. Judging by the lack of fear in his eyes, he knew it was going to be over soon. Mostly, he just looked tired.

Something about him made me stop and stare a little longer than I usually would have. I looked at his rifle lying a few feet from his side. His Luger was still attached to his belt, and I wondered whether I should take it from him. He was no longer a danger, though—whatever injury he'd sustained saw to that.

But still I looked at the Luger. It seemed like all the other guys wanted one, and here was my chance. I'd never had affection for guns, and I'd never joined in these taking-the-spoils rituals that followed German surrender. But for some reason, this time felt different. Perhaps I wanted something to make this war feel more human, more tangible. Strange as it may sound, even though part of me wanted to forget the war altogether, I think there was a part of me that wanted to be able to keep a piece of it in my pocket.

I didn't want a wristwatch, and I didn't want to be carrying around a German helmet for the rest of the war. Then I saw the ring on the man's finger. I pointed at it, hoping my German was close.

"Das ring," I said. "Bitte."

He lifted his hand. I reached out and felt the ring slide easily off his finger. I put the ring in my pocket.

"Danke," I said.

I left the ring in the box under my bed and pulled out my Bible. It was still too dark to read, but that didn't bother me much. I could recite by heart pretty much every passage I'd grown to rely on since leaving Camp Kilmer.

The pain in my leg spiked again, and I closed my eyes. I tried to remember all the different places where I'd read my Bible so far during this war. I saw a metal room filled with swaying hammocks as we crossed the Atlantic and timber-walled shacks with low cots as I waited to deploy from England. I remembered sitting by the docks, the smell of diesel fumes making me nauseous. I pictured countless beachheads and foxholes, wide-open fields, and thin forest clearings in the light of the early morning. Wherever I'd been, my Bible had been with me.

I must have drifted off to sleep, because the next time I opened my eyes it was light. The tent was bigger than I thought it would be, and I counted two rows of twelve beds facing each other and a doorway near my bed. The room was clean and calm, and every bed had a man lying quietly in it. The setting was almost peaceful, and despite the fact that there was nothing more than tarpaulin between us and the outside world, I felt safe. It was hard to believe I was outside Cherbourg, where we'd fought so hard against the Germans only a few months ago. A lot had changed since the summer.

The words of the thirty-seventh psalm drifted into my

mind, and I opened my Bible. As I took in the Scripture, it felt like peace was coursing through my lungs.

When the door opened, I looked up. A nurse walked in and went to the man in the bed opposite mine. She had her back to me, and I saw that she was short with thick, dark hair curling over the collar of her Army fatigues. It struck me that over the previous four days, I'd seen more American women than the number of hot meals I'd eaten in the previous five months. I was fascinated by the very sight of them, intrigued to find them here on the same soil that had been home to such brutality and fear.

When the nurse turned around, all thoughts of brutality, fear, my wounded leg, and the horrors of war exited from my mind. She was beautiful. There was a lightness about her—a sense of air and freedom and hope. Her eyes glowed with more life than seemed possible in a single human being. And she had a mouth that I didn't believe could be capable of forming anything but a smile.

All this I decided in the two seconds it took her to approach my bed. By the time she opened her mouth to say hello, I was caught, hook, line and sinker. As far as my heart was concerned, the deal was done. She was the one.

It was because of this sense of confidence that I didn't find her first words to me at all odd. She didn't talk to me about my leg or my general state of well-being; instead, she looked down at the Bible that was resting open on my chest and asked, "Are you a Christian?"

"Yes," I said.

"Really?" She delivered her words with a smile so bright that for a moment I wondered if someone was shining a flashlight on her face. "So am I!"

After that, I was done in. There was no way to contain my smile, no hope of squelching my joy. She asked about my leg, and I told her all about the 88 and the shrapnel and the Hürtgen Forest as if I were describing a trip up the Olentangy River to get ice cream and go swimming. In that moment, nothing was wrong in the world. Nothing could ever be wrong. Life was perfect and complete and simply wonderful.

She told me that I'd be operated on by Dr. Grodberg. "He's very good," she said. "He'll have you all fixed up right away."

I listened as she told me I'd be in the hospital for up to thirty days while I recovered. I listened to everything, but only for the joy of hearing her soft voice dance around in my head.

"My name's Lieutenant Carter," she said. I made a mental note to remember that.

Then she was gone, moving on to the next patient. I watched as she went from bed to bed, bringing a little bit of new life to each patient. I closed my eyes and sighed. *Bliss,* I thought. *This is what bliss feels like.*

It turned out that Lieutenant Carter was right: Dr. Grodberg was very good at his job. He sewed me up the next day, explaining as he worked what would happen to me. "It's a deep wound, all the way down to the bone, so it'll take a while to heal."

"As many as thirty days?" I asked.

"At least."

Perfect, I thought.

Lieutenant Carter was on the day shift that week, starting at seven o'clock and leaving twelve hours later. I returned from surgery and was happy just to be in the same tent with her, although I shared it with twenty-three other men. I was delighted when she came over to check on me and a little sad when her shift ended soon after.

I spent the night drifting in and out of musings about how wonderful she was. At some point, though, the course of my thoughts changed. It struck me that thirty days was not such a long time after all, and I'd already used up two of them. Thirty days was a long time in a foxhole, but the same was not true of a hospital. Time was speeding by, and soon I'd be gone.

This troubled me greatly, and the more I thought about it, the more daunting the problem became. Not only was time running out, but her rank of lieutenant made her an officer. I was just a staff sergeant, an enlisted man. Even if I recovered quickly enough to be able to move around and get out of the tent, what hope could I have of fraternizing with her?

I knew from my days in the Navy Air Corps that officers and enlisted men were separated by an invisible but unbreakable barrier. No matter how much I believed she was the one for me, there was no way she'd be able to get to know me. While I saw in her an angel of beauty, grace, and light, what would she see when she looked at me, other than just another wounded dogface?

As excited as I was to see Lieutenant Carter, seven o'clock came around too fast for my liking the next morning. I hadn't yet formulated a plan about how we could get to know each other, nor had I decided how I'd ever be able to tell if she liked me or not.

At some point during the night, I remembered standing in the Lazarus department store with Dale Jensen next to me, watching as he charmed his way into Colleen's affections. He'd told me that when the nation was at war, young lovers didn't wait around, and I drew comfort from the memory. Maybe thirty days—or twenty-seven, now—wasn't too short a time after all. But my happiness faded when I remembered Dale in his captain's uniform and how he'd talked about flying General Twining around. Compared to a captain, a staff sergeant didn't have much to brag about.

Lieutenant Carter soon came to my bedside, and we talked as she checked my leg. I was a little dumbstruck and perhaps too intent on reading her for signs of how she felt about me, but as she left I began to wonder, *Does she smile the same way at the other men?*

I strained to watch, although all I could see was her back. If she was smiling, the patient she was with must have been terribly sick, because his face was set in a stony scowl. There was no way a functioning human being could have resisted a full-on Lieutenant Carter smile.

I tried to listen for her voice. She was professional, polite, and friendly. There was no talk of Bibles, and there was no "me too" moment like she and I had shared the day before. Instead, she talked about the man's wound.

"I was shot in the foot," he said, his voice as bleak as his face.

"Oh," she said. "By a German?"

He didn't reply. It was obvious that his was a self-inflicted wound. I felt myself tense inside, remembering the stories I'd heard about men who had shown a similar lack of courage. Rumor had it that General Patton had accused one soldier of being a coward and then slapped him.

I had known fear, and I knew what cowardice tasted like. Every soldier did. But it was one of those bitter tastes you just had to swallow. Shooting yourself didn't just wound your own flesh; it left your fellow soldiers more vulnerable, putting them at even greater risk.

Just when I was about to disappear into a spiral of thoughts about cowardice, sacrifice, and honor, it happened. Lieutenant Carter turned away from the man with the wounded foot and looked back at me. And she smiled.

167th General Hospital
Cherbourg, France

December 20, 1944

Dear Mom and Dad,

Christmas came early when your parcel arrived. Those toilet paper rolls were about the best present a girl could get around here! I'm sorry I couldn't get you a present this year, but God willing, next Christmas I'll be home and I can make it up to you.

In many ways life carries on pretty much as normal. Dora, Peggy, Ruth, and I are working hard, and there are always new men to take care of and others to say goodbye to.

The weather has been cold—the coldest winter in memory, the locals say—and there's snow piled up high along the footpaths that link the tents. But even though we still haven't received our wool underwear and we're separated from the wind by nothing more than Army-issue tents, nobody seems to mind. None of us nurses have gotten ill. Isn't that amazing?

Some things are getting harder, though. This cold weather creates terrible conditions for the troops out there doing the fighting. We've seen more and more men coming in with trench foot, and we've had to open new wards to cope with the increase. The pain these men experience is unimaginable, yet they go through it with bravery and good grace you wouldn't believe.

Well, most of them do. We have one trench foot patient with us right now who shot himself in the foot. He's hoping that the bullet will do what the cold didn't manage and injure him so bad that he gets sent home. None of us girls have much respect for him. He lies in a ward where all the other men have put themselves in danger and risked their lives to fight for their squads and their country. I bet all of them have been scared and all of them have wanted the war to end, but unlike the coward with the hole in his foot, they chose to stay.

Still, we're here to treat and serve the men, no matter why they're here. I know God would want me to have compassion even for the ones with self-inflicted wounds. So I try. And I pray a lot and hope that somehow my frustration doesn't show.

There's been one other patient I've been looking after. His name's Whipps. He's the complete opposite of this other guy—brave and funny and kind. He's been here for two weeks, and he's like no other soldier I've met so far. He's a Christian and a really good man. I hope I'll be able to tell you more about him in my next letter.

With love to you both and to the boys,

Betty

167th General Hospital
Cherbourg, France

January 5, 1945

Dear Ray,

I think this is the first time I have ever used your Christian name. It's certainly the first time I've ever written to you. I've written about you before—I've added notes to your charts and such—but you've always been Staff Sergeant Whipps, just as I've always been Lieutenant Carter. In some ways, we've just been like any other nurse and her patient.

But something has happened between us. For the last twenty-nine days I haven't just been your nurse, helping you heal, watching you start to walk again. I've become your friend. And I'm so grateful for that. At a time when so many other men are coming into the hospital with a look that tells me they've seen things they're desperate to forget, you've brought light and life to the ward. So many times I've paused outside the tent and listened to you goofing off, making all the other fellas laugh. You really are going to be missed around here, Ray.

It's not just the guys either. I'm going to miss you. I'm going to miss talking about what life was like when we were growing up, finding out more about your family, and hearing about Columbus and Goffie and the things you did as a pilot.

I thank God for the fact that you didn't make it all the way through the Navy Air Corps. I don't think we would have met each other if you hadn't ended up in the Army. And I'm sorry you got hurt, but I have to say, in a way I'm thankful for it, because it meant you entered this makeshift hospital just a month ago.

I'm never going to send you this letter. It will stay hidden at the bottom of my trunk, away from all eyes but my own. I'm going to be especially careful to hide it from Major Leonard. I know that if she read it, I'd be in so much trouble with her. But in a way I suppose I'm also hiding it from you. I don't know if you feel the way that I do. I think you do. I hope you do. But now that you're getting better, you'll be redeployed soon. I don't know if you're thinking about the future or if you're just trying to get through the present.

I don't know how I'm ever going to find the courage to say goodbye to you tomorrow. This past month with you here has been wonderful. And it has left my head and heart spinning. I guess what I really want to say is this: I'm going to trust God for you. I'm going to trust that He'll take care of you, that He'll keep you safe, and that He'll bring you home.

Will that home include me? I don't know. But I'm going to trust that, if it's the right thing, God will continue what He has started between us. Even if tomorrow is our first and last goodbye, I'm going to trust that God holds us both in His hands.

Yours,
Betty

13

"I'LL WRITE TO YOU"

THERE HAD BEEN NO DOUBT IN MY MIND that as soon as day thirty came around, I'd have to leave the 167th General Hospital. I also knew that since I was still on crutches, I wouldn't be redeployed just yet. Even so, the news that I was shipping out to England the next morning felt as much like a blow as if an 88 had exploded at close range. There was someone I just wasn't ready to say goodbye to.

"Lieutenant Carter," I called as she entered the tent at the start of her night shift. As usual, a few of the guys in the tent whistled and cheered. Most of the time I just grinned and played it up when they teased me, but this time I had too much on my mind for joking around.

"I got my orders," I told her as she approached. This time her smile was a little less bright, her eyes a little less alive.

"Oh," she said. "And where are they sending you, Sergeant Whipps?"

"Oxford, England."

"Well, Dr. Grodberg did a great job, and your leg's healing well now. We've done about all we can for you here." She paused, and a half smile played its way onto her lips. "I'll miss you, Sergeant Whipps," she said quietly.

I knew how she felt. It was hard to believe we'd known each other just a few weeks. While I was bed-bound and we were getting to know each other, we'd stored up countless memories I'd take with me onto the battlefield. I'd never forget when Lieutenant Carter had one of the orderlies file down the calluses on my feet, and she and I counted the warts on our hands while he worked.

Once I was able to walk again, Betty accompanied me whenever she could—first on trips around the hospital and later to church. We sat side by side, struggling to concentrate on the sermon that was being preached. We even graduated to making a couple of trips to see a movie together, and again, I barely remembered what was being played on the screen in front of us. All my attention was focused on the beautiful girl sitting next to me. Nothing else mattered.

Of course, we were careful not to let on that we were spending time together, but the other nurses and the fellas in my ward weren't blind. They teased me more and more as the days ticked by, but I didn't mind so much. Every time they tried to embarrass me, my insides would light up with joy as I thought of Betty.

But that night—my last night before heading to England—was different. Not only would I be leaving Betty soon, but there had also been a sobering turn of events in the war. After the Germans had lost the battle for control of the Hürtgen Forest, they launched an offensive in another wooded area around the Ardennes. If the nature of the injuries of the wounded men pouring in was anything to go by, it was a brutal encounter, where the weather was just as dangerous a foe as the Germans.

Many of the men's feet were a deathly gray color, as if all the life had been sucked out of them, and they were swollen, too. The skin on some of the soldiers was peeling off, and from a few men came a smell that was all too familiar to anyone who had been around dead bodies. Other men had been hit by shrapnel or bullets, like the rest of us, but what stood out about nearly all those who had been injured in the Ardennes was their demeanor. When they weren't crying out in pain, they were quiet, their eyes vacant. They wouldn't be able to forget what they'd seen.

That last night in the hospital, I had my own troubles to deal with. New patients had come in during the day, and Lieutenant Carter was busy tending to them, meaning we barely had time to talk. Not that I could have said what I wanted to say from a hospital bed anyway.

I don't remember sleeping much that night. Mostly I just sat on my bed rehearsing what I wanted to say to Lieutenant Carter. As the walls of the tent began to brighten, I stopped measuring the time I had left with her in hours and started counting down the minutes.

I watched as she moved around the tent, making her last checks on patients before her shift ended. She moved with grace and kindness among the beds, just as she always had. I watched her make her way down the line, one patient at a time, toward me. When she reached me, there was nothing either of us could say except that one dreaded word: "Goodbye."

The moment seven o'clock struck, a nurse walked in through the doors, ready to relieve Lieutenant Carter. I saw them talk awhile and then watched Lieutenant Carter leave. But I wasn't in my bed. I was leaning on my crutches on the other side of the doorway.

She smiled when she saw me waiting for her outside the tent. I knew that we had no time to waste and that if we were caught, she'd be the one who would suffer the consequences. So I skipped straight to the point.

"Betty," I said, using her Christian name for the first time, "if we get out of this, will you marry me?"

As I watched her face, the word that came to mind was *resplendent*. She was always beautiful, but this was the most beautiful I'd ever seen her. Her eyes danced and her smile grew.

"Yes," she said.

"I'd like you to have this," I said, pulling the simple gold ring out of my pocket.

She looked at it resting in the palm of my hand, then back at me before reaching out and taking it.

"I'd like that," she said. I decided to wait to tell her how I got the ring.

The noise of someone approaching reminded us how little time we had.

"I'll write to you," she said, reaching out to hold my hand for the briefest of seconds.

"I'd like that," I said.

And then she was gone. I watched her walk away down a path with snow piled high on either side. When she disappeared from view, I drifted back into the tent. I got a little cheer from the guys, but since nobody had seen what happened on the other side of the doorway, they didn't know there really was cause for celebration. That was okay with me. I had some planning to do.

By the time I arrived in England toward the end of the day, I knew what I had to do. Christmas had come and gone, and the war was still very much in force. At this rate, I thought, it could carry on for another year or more. Even if the Germans surrendered, the fighting in the Pacific was still raging. I could be redeployed anywhere, and so could Betty. The only chance we had of being together was if I took whatever leave was offered me and traveled to meet her.

It was the only possible solution I could come up with, but it didn't solve that old hurdle we'd faced all along: lieutenants simply weren't allowed to fraternize with enlisted men. If this plan of meeting up while on leave was going to work, I would have to become an officer.

I was moved to a hospital on the outskirts of Oxford, where I was encouraged to go on frequent walks around the city and the surrounding villages to help rebuild strength in my leg. I ambled around so many ancient colleges and quaint country villages that I almost forgot I was a soldier who'd been sent thousands of miles from home to fight a war.

Almost, but not quite. Because no matter how much history or beauty I saw, I couldn't ignore the fact that I was going to be redeployed. Not that I didn't want to return to the action—I had no desire to flee or renege on my responsibilities—but things were different now. I had a reason to make it out alive.

My faith had helped me in so many ways throughout the war. Whenever I prayed and read my Bible, God had given me reassurance, and even when shells fell near me, I wasn't really afraid of death. I never liked the thought of dying, but I knew they could kill only my body, not my soul. Although I wasn't in a hurry to get to heaven, I didn't spend much time worrying about whether my life would be cut short.

Now, however, things looked different. Those 88s and German snipers were not a shortcut to heaven; they were a threat to the life I hoped to spend with the woman I was in love with.

All this weighed on me as I walked the streets, lanes, and fields around Oxford throughout January and into February. At first I was on crutches, but I was told to get rid of them as soon as possible and start walking free again. Eventually the muscles and tissue repaired well enough for me to walk without feeling too much pain. The stronger I got, the heavier my sense of dread became—so much so that when I was finally told that I was going back to join the Fourth Division, the news came as something of a relief.

I was shipped from Southampton to France, and over the next couple of days I took a series of trucks that made up the Red Ball Express and crossed over the country to Nancy. There, at Army headquarters, I took an exam to see whether I could apply for officer training. Thankfully, there wasn't much high-level math, and the questions on geography and leadership didn't trouble me. Before I left the city, I was told I'd passed and was invited to join the next training class on April 1, almost six weeks away.

The Red Ball Express took me north again to meet up with the rest of the Fourth Division. I was not alone on these drives, but I might as well have been. My thoughts were heavy with the anticipation of what was coming next: the feel of a rifle in my hands, the weight of a pack on my back, the sound of artillery exploding close at hand. All these would be waiting for me when I rejoined the

Twenty-Second, and sooner or later they would become normal again.

From time to time I'd look at my fellow passengers. Most of them were replacements, first-timers who had yet to fire their weapons in danger. You could always tell. All you had to do was look into their eyes and see the fear running wild.

Arriving a few miles behind the line, I reported to the major of the division. "Are you ready?" he asked.

"Yes, sir."

"Good. We'll send you back to the same squad in C company, and you can take over there. You're being promoted to tech sergeant." It was a bump up a grade, and I was happy about it. I still wasn't an officer, but it was a step in the right direction toward officer training. Once that was out of the way, I'd be able to spend time with Betty again. Nothing else mattered.

167th General Hospital
Cherbourg, France

January 6, 1945

Dear Mom and Dad,

Remember the guy I mentioned in my last letter? Well,
yesterday he proposed! I'm engaged, and you've got yourselves
a future son-in-law! I'm so happy, and I wish I could be telling
you this in person so you could see the grin that's stuck to
my face.

His name is Ray Whipps, and he's a staff sergeant. He's
a wonderful man. I think he must be the smartest, kindest,
funniest, and most upright man in the whole Army. You're
going to love him so much, Mom and Dad.

He was here at the hospital for thirty days after his leg
was wounded. He was quite badly cut up, with the laceration
going almost all the way to the bone, but Dr. Grodberg did a
great job putting him back together. Throughout Ray's time
here, no matter how much pain he was in, he never seemed
to complain. He was always laughing and goofing off in the
ward. He's so like his name—a ray of light that brightens up
even the darkness of war. When he laughs, it's impossible
not to get caught up in it and laugh along with him. He's a
Christian too, so we've been to church together a couple
of times. He's kind and thoughtful, and he's just a good,
moral man. And he happens to be the best-looking GI you've
ever seen!

Ray and I started talking when I saw him reading his
Bible. In all the months I've been here, I'd never seen another
soldier reading Scripture, even though there are plenty of us
nurses who rely on it to get us through. Ray and I talked about
God and church and how Scripture can be such a support,
especially in times like these.

In many ways, that first conversation never really stopped.
In the month he was here, we kept talking about life and God

and what it means to trust Him even when our plans don't seem to be working out.

Like me, Ray had initial plans that just didn't work out. He started out training to be a pilot in the Navy Air Corps, but after a series of circumstances out of his control, he ended up as an infantryman. We both know what it feels like to be bitterly disappointed, but also for that disappointment to fade over time as we learn to trust God a little more.

Ray left the hospital yesterday, and he's going back to England to recuperate some more. In time I guess he'll be back out with his men. I'm wearing the ring he gave me on my dog collar chain, because if Major Leonard finds out, I'll be in real trouble.

But the girls have been great. They've listened to me as I've told them all about how great Ray is, and they know how hard it was to say goodbye. They've also been kind as I'm dealing with so many fears for his safety once he's redeployed.

For the first time since 1941, I'm praying that the war ends quickly and that we can all get home again.

With love,
Betty

14

NO REST FOR THE WEARY

I KNEW FROM THE MEN I'D SEEN carried into the 167th
General Hospital that the fighting throughout December
had been costly, but I had no idea quite how bad it had
been. As I drew closer to the fighting, I heard more about
the Battle of the Bulge and the conditions the soldiers there
had faced. Even so, I was surprised when I arrived up at the
line and found my squad. There was nobody in it I recognized. Not a single person.

I looked around the other two squads in the platoon,
and again, nobody looked familiar. I asked whether anyone
knew where Anders was, but all I received were blank faces
and shrugged shoulders. In the two and a half months since

I'd left the Twenty-Second, every one of the fifty men in my platoon had been killed, captured, or seriously wounded.

In addition to the new men in my squad, I also had a new officer above me. Lieutenant Olsen was young, but judging by the way he shouted orders at people, he was confident enough.

"Tech Sergeant Whipps," he said after I'd introduced myself, "your squad's on guard duty tonight."

My squad was almost at full strength, and out of the ten, I chose two privates first class for duty. It was strange, but I slept well, curled up under my raincoat and finally wearing the winter uniform the Army had supplied. More than two months of sleeping on a proper bed hadn't robbed me of the ability to sleep like a true dogface.

I woke up with a pair of boots in front of my face and a volley of shouts filling my ears. It was still dark, but dawn wasn't far off. Standing over me was Lieutenant Olsen.

"On your feet, Tech Sergeant Whipps," he barked.

I jumped up and asked what was going on. Beside him, shoulders slumped and looking like he was about to start crying, was one of the young soldiers I'd put on guard duty.

"Your man here," Olsen said, prodding the young private first class in the chest with his gloved hand, "took it upon himself to fall asleep during guard duty." He paused, and I wondered if I should say something. The truth was, though I hadn't forgotten how to go to sleep like an infantryman, I had yet to remember how to wake up as quickly as one. I tried to will myself fully awake.

"You do know that in some instances this soldier could be killed for something like this, don't you?"

I said that I did and that I'd make sure it wouldn't happen again.

"Well, that's irrelevant. I'm taking the squad away from you. I won't take away your rank, but know that I could."

"Yes, sir."

He marched away, taking the terrified-looking soldier with him.

It did not trouble me that I'd lost charge of my squad. I'd had enough experience leading men in the months before I was injured to know that I could do it, and I didn't need a title to prove it. But over the next two days, as we engaged the Germans in fast-moving battles across wide-open spaces, I quickly felt frustrated. The corporal whom Olsen had placed in charge of the squad wasn't giving the strong leadership that the less-experienced replacement troops needed. He was hanging back when it was time to move forward, staying silent when he should have been calling out instructions. So it was something of a relief when, at the end of the second day of the corporal leading the squad, Olsen called me over.

"Whipps," he said, barely looking up from the map he was studying, "I'm putting you back in charge of the squad."

"Yes, sir."

I respected Olsen as someone in authority over me, but I struggled with his decisions, which often led us into greater risk than necessary. One day as we moved from the wide-open country into a more forested area, he called on me to go in among the trees and down a firebreak to see if I could tell whether there was a German sniper hiding in a fire tower.

"You're fast," he said. "So it won't be a problem for you."

I went alone into the forest. It was cold and a little dark, and I couldn't help but think of the days I'd spent in the Hürtgen Forest. I kept low, using the trees as cover, keeping my eyes and ears on high alert.

After twenty minutes, I was far enough in to be able to see the fire tower, about thirty yards ahead. It was tall—twenty or thirty feet up—and set in the middle of the firebreak. If I wanted a clear look at it, all I had to do was step out into the clear, but there was no chance of my doing that. Instead, I tried to move as silently as possible into a position where I could see inside the tower.

As soon as I caught sight of the sniper, I heard a noise among the trees near me. It was an elk, the biggest one I'd ever seen. I was already standing perfectly still, and it took a moment for the animal to notice me. Once it did, it froze too. We both stayed there, locked in a stare for what felt like minutes. I hoped it wouldn't startle and run away, drawing the sniper's attention. The elk probably had questions of its own, wondering why I wasn't attacking.

Eventually the animal slipped away, not as silently as I'd hoped, but quietly enough. When I was sure the sniper hadn't noticed, I inched back toward our men, relieved that Olsen's plan hadn't backfired.

★

I didn't know if it was because the Germans felt that the war was slipping from their grasp, but by March 1945, we were taking more prisoners. Instead of digging in and fighting off our attacks as they had in the Hürtgen Forest, they surrendered more easily. As we pushed farther east, we started to see groups of German soldiers sitting by the side of the road or riding in trucks passing the other way, always watched closely by Allied soldiers. While the soldiers we'd encountered at Saint-Lô were young, healthy, and well trained, we were now fighting those who had previously been considered too old or too young. These were the last and the least, and most of them didn't look like they wanted to die for Hitler's cause.

Regardless of what the German elite believed, we knew the war was coming to an end. Of course, we'd felt the same way at the end of summer, after Paris had fallen, but somehow this was different. The Luftwaffe had been largely immobilized, and their air attacks had dropped off. Hürtgen Forest and the Battle of the Bulge had proved that no matter how tightly the Germans clung to their positions, given enough time—and enough men—we would win.

Day after day we pushed east. We weren't without casualties, but the German defense had slackened considerably. On the last day of February 1945, we broke through the German line near Olzheim. A week later we crossed the Kyll River, a dozen miles farther into Germany. We were given a week's break from the front and returned to France before resuming our operations in Haguenau, ten miles from the Rhine River.

It was strange to be fighting our way from France into Germany again, but the sight of the Rhine, flowing fast and wide beneath a cloudy sky, only made us more determined to push ahead and win this war. The only bridge within miles had been mined, and our combat engineers had laid a pontoon bridge across the water. We walked across, believing there was nothing the Germans could do to stop us.

Our days were marked by a new but familiar routine. Instead of sleeping in foxholes, we made our beds in open fields or empty farm buildings. Instead of eating our cold K rations huddled beneath fallen trees, we sat with our backs against solid brick buildings and our legs stretched out before us. We moved out at our own pace and spent our days overpowering German squads and sweeping through villages, where we checked for soldiers in hiding. We were like a flood moving steadily forward—never reversing, always pulsing ahead.

March 31 started just like any other day. We'd spent the night in yet another farmyard, and I woke up to the familiar feeling of soft ground beneath me. Lieutenant Olsen had chosen to sleep in the house itself, and judging by the look on the elderly owners' faces, they hadn't appreciated being thrown out into the barn.

It was dry, and the sky was perfectly clear. I thought about Betty as I ate my breakfast, wondering what she was doing right then. I thought about the ring I'd left her with and felt a hint of sorrow that there had been no time for her to fetch a keepsake for me. What I would have given to have a photo of her to put in my breast pocket beside my Bible.

I led my squad as we moved out for our next set of battles. It was a typical day of fighting, made up of sporadic skirmishes with the handful of Germans we found. There were no pillboxes or machine gun nests for them to hide in, and the squat farmhouses gave their snipers limited vantage points. A few were determined to fight, but for the most part they were moving back at the same pace we were, as if this were a childhood race for the safety of home.

By the time the light started to fade and the day's fighting ended, we settled into our usual routines: taking turns on guard duty, reading and writing letters, burning our K-ration boxes to heat our meals. Most of us sat quietly, preoccupied with our own thoughts. Mine, as ever, were of Betty.

We were making enough progress that we could relax a bit, but we weren't far enough into Germany to start believing that victory was imminent. A strange mood settled on us—not quite calm, but the deep tiredness that comes at the end of a hard day's work. We knew this rest would offer only temporary relief before the next day's labors began.

Though we'd looked for a farmhouse to sleep in, we hadn't found one in the last hour or so of fighting. We'd stopped at the edge of a field, but Lieutenant Olsen wasn't happy about these sleeping conditions. As the others ate, he called the three squad leaders.

"We're not staying here," he said. "There's a town one mile ahead, and we're going to take it."

"The men are tired, sir." I said.

I wished I could say more—I wanted to tell him that this was a foolish idea and that we'd never fought all day and then kept fighting into the night. Besides the fact that this was asking too much of the men, there was no need for such a push. We had the Germans on the run, and we were moving ahead just as we needed to. I couldn't see any reason for fighting through the night other than to find Lieutenant Olsen a nice bed to sleep in at the end of it.

He waved me aside and instructed his radio man to call and ask for permission to keep moving. A few seconds later he had it, and I had no choice but to go and tell my men.

There's no tiredness quite as heavy as the kind that settles on you after the prospect of a full night's sleep has been taken away. As we shouldered our gear and prepared to take the town, I knew this was too much for my squad. There were enough surprises in war as it was, and having to switch from eating chow and getting ready for bed to being ready to hunt out the enemy was the kind of surprise no soldier relished. Truth be told, I was struggling too. My leg had been throbbing ever since we broke into Germany, and I was concerned about how it would feel after another few hours of walking, falling to the ground, and pushing off quickly again.

Olsen had assured us that the town was small and that we'd clear it quickly, but from the very beginning, things were more complicated than we'd expected. My squad was told to approach along the south side of a ravine, which was allegedly clear farmland. However, even in the half-moonlight, it was obvious that this was not the case. Wide-limbed trees spread across the slope, casting long, black shadows over the ground below.

We spread out in a line, with me at the bottom of the ravine. It was even darker there, and I had to concentrate on each step to find steady ground to walk on. I was still wary of my leg, and the last thing I wanted to do was trip and fall.

Between the uneven ground, the darkness, the weight of all my equipment, and the lack of sleep, I started to lose focus. I began to feel frustrated with the position we were in. After a day of chasing German soldiers eastward, we should have been back in the field resting up for the night, not inching our way across the German countryside.

I was convinced we were making a mistake. Simple errors can easily leak into a platoon when the end of the war feels close. I knew there were too many lives at stake to delay unnecessarily, and I knew it was our God-given duty to act, yet in this case Olsen hadn't sent us out to save lives. He'd sent us out to save himself from getting a sore back.

I never should have allowed myself to drift so far off into these thoughts, and I never should have allowed myself to become separated from the rest of my men, but when I looked up and scanned the tree line for the familiar shapes of my squad, they were gone. I held my breath and listened, hoping to hear a footstep or the faintest hint of a whisper. Nothing.

I moved up the hill, hoping to find them on the other side, but even though the trees thinned out as the hill fell away, I couldn't see any of them.

My second mistake came quickly after that. I stumbled along the top of the ridge for what felt like an hour before dropping down into the town I was sure we were heading for. Passing through a field, I could see buildings ahead, but not enough to constitute anything more than a small village. Even so, I convinced myself that this was the place Olsen had meant. There were no lights in any of the windows, but I was sure that inside one of the buildings I'd find the rest of my men waiting for me.

I knocked on the door. The voice that came from inside was muffled and sounded nothing like that of a US soldier, but I thought it must have been a private I'd barely spoken to before. I was wrong.

The door opened to reveal an old man—an old German man—and a young girl.

After that, my mistakes came thick and fast. In halting German, I asked them where the Americans were. They looked scared but said they hadn't seen any. I pushed into the house and tried another question.

"Wo sind der Deutsche soldaten?"

Again they both shook their heads and said they did not know of any.

I asked if there were other people in the village.

"Ja."

"Bring them here," I said, giving up on German.

They understood enough and both walked toward the door.

"Not her." I pointed at the girl. I was tired and making mistakes, but I didn't want them thinking they could escape. "She stays here. She'll be safe."

The old man left and I exhaled. It was warm inside, and as I waited for him to return, I felt the last of my energy draining from my body. The girl stood in a corner, her eyes on me the whole time. I took off my helmet and tried to rub some of the pain from my leg.

When the old man returned, he brought six or seven others with him. They were all elderly, and most of them were women.

There was one young man, though, and I must have looked at him strangely, because he looked me in the eye and said, "American?"

"Yes."

"Polish," he said, tapping his chest.

"I'm tired," I said. "Do you understand that?"

"Yes."

"I need to sleep. Where can I go?"

"You can sleep in barn," he said. "You can lock door."

I didn't bother to weigh the wisdom of this idea or question whether he was telling the truth. I was exhausted, and he had given me a solution. That was all I needed to know.

"You all stay in here tonight," I said, waving my rifle around a little. "I'm going to sleep."

I left the house and found the barn. The doors were heavy, but once I'd swung them shut, I couldn't find a lock or bar to keep them closed. By that point I was utterly spent. I'd had enough of mud and weapons, of fighting and fear for one day. I was beyond caring what dangers would be prowling nearby while I rested. I just needed it all to stop.

In the darkness, I felt my way to a patch of straw I'd glimpsed when the door was open. I dropped the pack from my back, placed my helmet and M1 rifle to the side, and lay down. On instinct, I checked my breast pocket for my Bible, and though it was too dark to read, I held it in my hands. The comforting smell of the pages took my mind off the barn's unfamiliar odors: cold metal, ancient timber, and rotting straw. I'd been weary before, but this exhaustion that was overtaking me was new. I could barely move—I felt like someone had mixed sawdust into my blood.

In the seconds before sleep came, I wondered how I'd ended up like this. I was supposed to be a pilot, high above this scrambling along the ground. Instead of soaring in the sky, I'd spent every day of the war burrowed into the soil. Like an animal, I'd learned to find safety in the earth, digging away from danger, letting fear drive my arms as they flung the shovel into the mud time and time again. It hadn't always worked. My hand and my leg still bore the scars and the pain to prove it.

But as much as I wouldn't have chosen this path, I was thankful for the unexpected good that came of it. Although the war brought me face-to-face with death, it had also given me a reason to make it out alive. In the eyes of that beautiful, smiling, God-loving nurse, I'd found an answer to the one question that had been troubling me more than any other: Why had God led me down this strange path?

My dreams were agitated and disjointed that night. My mind flashed with half-formed images of bloodied hands, torn flesh, gray smoke, a young man crying with fear. In the next instant, I was flying in the hills above Spokane, feeling the late-afternoon sun on my face. Then she was there—the nurse—her eyes, her smile, and her words warming my face. And all at once, someone I couldn't see began to clap.

The clapping grew louder, then louder still. There was something wrong with it, something that didn't quite fit. I woke up. It was still dark, but the barn felt different. Another clap shattered the air, then one more, and another after that. They were bullets. Instinctively I pushed myself lower into the hay, reaching for my rifle as I did so. The exhaustion had left, but in its place was a new feeling, as if my blood were mixed with acid. I tasted metal, but I couldn't swallow.

At the far end of the barn I saw faint light from outside falling through the freshly torn bullet holes. There was a moment of quiet. Then a German voice called out orders I didn't understand. The claps resumed, with new holes appearing in the barn wall, each getting closer to where I lay.

If I stayed in the straw, the gunshots would reach me within seconds. There was nothing else I could do but fill my lungs with air, lift my head, and shout.

"Comrade! I surrender!"

167th General Hospital
Cherbourg, France

March 29, 1945

Dearest Ray,

I hope that you got my letter from the weekend and that you could read my writing. It was dark and cold when I wrote it, and I was struggling to see the page clearly. But it is a little warmer today, and I have enough time to write before the light fades.

Even though I know it's difficult for you to reply, it's good to be able to share some of my most precious memories with you in these letters. Dora and Peggy keep teasing me about the amount of detail I'm sharing with you, but I think they understand, really. And this morning at breakfast, when they asked me what I was going to write to you about today, they told me I really ought to tell you less about how I used to fight with my three little brothers and more about how if anyone ever tried to take them on I'd defend them like a lioness.

I think the people I want to write about today are my grandparents. Grandpa Carter was a farmer, and he and Grandma Carter were just what you'd imagine a set of farming grandparents to look like. The Depression was tough on them. We couldn't travel to see them as much as we liked, and they were tied to the farm back in Iowa. When I was in the third grade, Grandma Carter died of a heart attack when she was helping fight a fire. It was a sad time for everyone, especially Grandpa Carter, but we were happy he moved in with us after the funeral. Having him in the house was so special.

We were never allowed to call Grandpa Ebbert "Grandpa." He has always been "Dad Ebbert," and he still has a head full of jet-black hair. Grandma Ebbert was one of the dearest, sweetest little ladies you could ever find. You think I'm short—well, Grandma Ebbert could fit under my arm! She used to work circles around everyone and made the most amazing chokecherry jelly and fresh rolls.

All of us kids thought she and Dad Ebbert were millionaires. Every summer they visited us from North Dakota, and they always had a nice car and bought us ice-cream cones. But what I remember most about Dad Ebbert was the way he encouraged me to do my very best. He always sat with me and told me how proud he was of me. The thing is, I know he was disappointed I wasn't a boy. He and Grandma Ebbert had seven girls and one boy, but the boy died when he was only a few days old. I was their first grandchild, and I know they were hoping for a boy. But knowing that just made his kind words and encouragement all the more special to me.

Both sets of grandparents taught us to persevere and not give up. I guess that was the only option back then. Even though the Depression was hard on my parents, we didn't really feel we had a hard life or anything. I only had one dress to wear, and the only thing between the ground and my feet was flimsy cardboard. Every time I came home for lunch, I'd get more cardboard to put in the bottom of my shoes, hoping it would last the rest of the day.

Dad never took a vacation. On weekends he would take all four of us kids out and let Mother get the Sunday dinner ready. Dad had always wanted to drive a train or be an engineer, and he loved the airport, the train station, and the ship harbor. He'd take us to one of those spots and buy a bag of bananas or hamburgers for us to eat as we watched the giant machines move in front of us.

As for me, I always wanted to be a nurse like Aunt Jo. She was an old maid, and she worked as a missionary in Argentina. She was over six feet tall, and everybody loved her. I thought everything about her was wonderful, and I wanted to be just like her one day. I had my sights set on being a missionary in either Alaska or Africa. Before the war, that's all I ever wanted to do with my life. After Pearl Harbor, I knew I was supposed to take that dream of being a nurse to help soldiers in the war instead.

It's funny, but writing about the Depression reminded me of what life was like in nurses' training. There were only ten of us at first, but we did everything together. We'd happily share one dill pickle or one milkshake, and people said our class had more fun on no money than anyone else. We had the most wonderful nursing arts instructor who instilled good ethics into us. She helped me see nursing in a new way, urging me to do my best just as Dad Ebbert had encouraged me to do.

The other day someone asked me where you and I are going to live when we get married, and I realized I don't know. Wherever you want to live will be just fine with me. Just as long as we have six daughters!

I've got to stop now, as my shift will be starting soon. Know that I'm praying for you whenever I can. I pray when I'm working, when I'm walking, and when I'm eating. Not an hour goes by that I don't ask God to keep you safe and reunite us again so we can begin to build our life together.

With love,
Betty

15

NO WAY OUT . . . ALIVE

"What division are you in?"

The German soldier towered over me, his oversized hands jabbing at my chest.

It was still dark outside—too dark to see what was going on in the shadows around me. I was confused and cold. My head was still ringing after the volley of bullets, and my insides felt as though they'd been hollowed out.

The question came again, only now there was more force in the heavily accented voice. "What division are you in?"

On instinct, I looked at the speaker's uniform, checking his collar for the telltale insignia that would mark him as a member of the SS. I found none.

"Tech Sergeant Whipps. 35 292 615."

I looked at the man's face. He wasn't much older than me, but he was taller. His eyes were deep set and hard to see under the peak of his helmet. He leaned in closer, and I smelled a touch of liquor and tobacco on his breath.

An officer? I wondered.

Again he asked the question, and again I remembered the simple instruction from basic training: tell them your name, rank, and serial number—and nothing else.

"Tech Sergeant Whipps. 35 292 615."

He stepped back to confer with another soldier. The two of them exchanged a few words, but they spoke too quietly and quickly for me to understand. Both men looked at me, and I watched as the officer dropped his hand to his belt, unfastened a strap, and brought out a knife. He called out an order, and two other soldiers appeared at my side.

I hadn't been wearing my pack when they found me in the barn, but my pockets were still full of all the items I typically carried with me: a small first-aid kit, some matches, a little food, the photo and letters from home, and the letters from Betty. The soldiers pulled everything out of my pockets, making no effort to treat me gently. I tried not to offer any resistance—I figured it was best for them to think I was no threat.

I watched them examine everything they pulled out. I didn't see my Bible anywhere, and I hoped that somehow they'd missed it. Then I remembered I'd fallen asleep with it on my chest. I guessed it was still back in the barn.

These thoughts distracted me from the fact that the officer was still holding his knife. I looked at him, and the blade flashed as he lifted it up to neck height. He held it there and started walking toward me.

I'd never really thought about what it would feel like to die or to be plunged into great pain. Most of the time in battle, death and pain sneak up on people without much warning. But this was different. I looked from the knife to the officer's face, trying to fathom what he was going to do.

Silent prayers echoed within me. *Lord, please protect me. Keep me safe.*

The blade dropped a little as the officer reached me. His left hand reached out and grabbed my shoulder while his right hand brought the knife toward me. I closed my eyes and waited for the pain, but it didn't come. Instead, I felt him tugging at my sleeve.

I opened my eyes. He had removed my insignia—that was all.

The officer backed away, disappearing from view. I let my head drop and silently thanked God. I knew the soldiers were all watching me, making sure I didn't try to escape. I wondered what would come next.

Minutes passed before the officer returned, holding my insignia. "You're in the Fourth Division, and you're in the Twenty-Second Infantry," he said. "But I'm not sure which company you are with."

I was impressed, though I set my face to stone and tried not to show any reaction at all.

"Where are the rest of your men? Why were you in this barn? What are your orders?"

The questions kept coming, but each time I stayed silent. I looked at the ground when I could, but when he forced me to look at him, I focused my eyes on a dented spot at the peak of his helmet. From time to time I repeated my name, rank, and serial number, but mostly I acted as if I couldn't understand him at all. It wasn't as hard to do this as I thought it would be. All I had to do was concentrate on how tired I felt, and I could feel the courtyard slipping away from me.

Eventually the questions stopped.

I hadn't noticed the sky starting to get light, but when a German soldier pushed some K rations in front of me, I saw that it was nearly dawn. The soldier motioned for me to sit. I slumped down, right where I'd spent the last few hours on my feet. The relief was sweet.

I looked around and counted more than a dozen soldiers, none of them wearing anything to mark them as members of the SS. The handful of buildings surrounding us were all intact, unscarred by the war, and as I ate my food, I noticed a few of the villagers walking around. There was one face I immediately recognized: it was the Polish man who had told me to sleep in the barn. The Germans had him bring me my water canteen, and though I tried to catch his eye, he wouldn't meet my gaze. I guessed that he was the one who had told the soldiers about me. I couldn't blame him, though. I knew I would have done the same in his position.

When the officer returned and a soldier pulled me to my feet, I staggered, almost losing my balance.

"We have soldiers going back to the next town," he said, ignoring my struggle to stand. "You will go with them, and then you will be sent to a prisoner-of-war camp or to prison. But first, we have some work for you."

I was taken to the side of the barn, where there was a small pile of pots and pans. I was largely ignored as I went about the task of cleaning them. Once I'd finished, the officer's boots appeared in front of me. I polished them as well.

When I was told that we were about to leave the village, I struggled to my feet again. My leg felt worse, and I calculated that I could have slept for only one or two hours in the barn. I reminded myself that all I needed to do was take one step, then another. That was my job.

Flanked by five soldiers, I walked down narrow lanes that snaked around the base of a steep hill. I thought about how I'd gotten lost the night before and wondered how far I was from the rest of my platoon. I tried listening for the sound of weapons, but I couldn't hear anything. The soldiers were so relaxed and the air was so quiet that we might as well have been fifty miles from the fighting.

As I thought through the events of the night before, I was reminded of the date. It was April 1, 1945—the day I was supposed to be in Paris beginning my officer training.

I wondered why the order to report there hadn't come in earlier when I'd been with the Twenty-Second. Had the message not gotten through? Had the plans for the training changed? Somehow it didn't seem to matter so much anymore.

The Germans heard the sound of the plane before I did. They stopped, looked behind us, and shouted. There was little cover around—no trees close by and no tall hedgerows like in Normandy—but a little way ahead was a truck, parked at the edge of a field. Strong hands grabbed me and hauled me along with the others as we ran for the truck. We threw ourselves facedown beneath it.

The engines were loud, and the planes were flying fast and low. I didn't need to look up to know that they were our P-47s, two of them. They fired a line of bullets along the road, some spitting up stone from the track beside us, others hitting the truck above. I felt the familiar sting of shrapnel as it bit into one of my fingers, but there was no time to assess the damage and no chance of sympathy from the Germans. As soon as the planes had gone, we started marching again, a little faster this time.

My hand was cut up, but it wasn't bad enough to distract me from the aching tiredness in every muscle and every bone. The soldiers just wanted to get me to the town quickly, and I struggled to keep up with them. Yet they weren't unkind to me, and for the most part they let me stumble along, slowing down for me when I needed to rest.

After an hour or two, the fields gave way to houses as

we approached the town. Once again, I was struck by how little the war had touched these places. The fighting had left much of France, Belgium, and Luxembourg in ruins, yet inside Germany, it was almost as if life had carried on as usual. Well-dressed women of all ages, old men, and young children moved through the streets as if the war were taking place a whole continent away. It was a strange sight, and for a moment I forgot my body's complaints.

Up ahead, coming from what looked like the main town square, I saw a motorbike with a sidecar approach. It was going fast, but it slowed and eventually stopped on the other side of the road. The soldiers I was with stopped walking and seemed to tense up, and instinctively I tried to make myself less conspicuous, shuffling behind my captors and willing myself to stay small.

The sergeant was called over to the motorbike and saluted whoever was in the sidecar. I shifted to get a better look. Based on his cap and the insignia on his collar, I could tell he was an SS officer. His eyes met mine, and I shrank back as best as I could, but it was too late. The SS officer rattled off what sounded like a series of orders, and when I snuck a quick glance at him again, I saw him pointing at me.

The motorbike's engine kicked in again, taking the officer away.

"Do you know who that was?" the sergeant asked me in surprisingly good English.

"I have a pretty good idea," I said.

"I'm supposed to turn you in at the SS headquarters in this town."

I felt my stomach wrench into a knot.

The sergeant paused before he spoke again. "I don't like them any better than you do. So I'm not going to do it."

I didn't say anything, but inside I was cheering. We kept walking, but with every step we took toward the town, the fear grew within me. What if we saw the SS officer again? What if one of the other soldiers decided he didn't want to disobey the order and chose to hand me over himself? What if we saw other SS when we reached the town?

Head down, eyes locked on the ground, I took each step knowing that at any moment I could be stopped and taken.

Lord God, I prayed silently, *if it hadn't been for your help and protection, I'd be dead already. Please don't let that happen now.*

We approached a low building with a heavy door. From the outside I could hear the sounds of men shouting. I must have looked terrified, because the sergeant smiled at me and said, "We're going in here now. It is good inside."

In some ways, he was right. On the other side of the door was a tavern with long benches. The room was warm and filled with more than twenty men, all drinking beer and looking relaxed. The trouble was that they were all German soldiers.

The sergeant, noticing how tense I was, gave me a friendly push that propelled me inside. I waited for the men to fall silent as they noticed my presence, but if they spotted me, they didn't show it. They just kept drinking and laughing as if this were a typical Friday evening at the end of a long workweek.

"Drink," the sergeant said, placing a large glass of beer in front of me. I'd never drunk alcohol before, and there was no way I was going to start now. Between the SS outside and a room full of German soldiers, I figured I'd need all my wits about me.

"Nein, danke," I said.

Neither the sergeant nor any of the other men could believe it, but after a few attempts at getting me to change my mind, they went back to the business of draining their own glasses. I sat still, hoping they'd move me to someplace safer soon. I kept an eye on the door and checked every person who came through it to see if they were SS. I tried to think about how I could escape, but with only one door in the tavern, I simply couldn't come up with a plan.

After an hour and more empty beer glasses on the table than I could count, we left. I was handed over to another squad that was camping out in what looked like an old school. It was nowhere near dark, but I lay down and slept, knowing I needed all the energy I could muster.

The next day, I was feeling a little better as we started our march. My new captors didn't seem to speak any English, and I was content to blend into the background as much as possible. My uniform marked me as an outsider, and there was nothing I could do about that, but at least if people weren't talking to me, I could hope to avoid any unnecessary attention.

I didn't know what I'd find when I ended up at the prisoner-of-war camp or the prison—assuming the plans for me hadn't changed—but I knew that whatever I had to face behind bars, at least I'd be packed in with other Allied soldiers. That had to be better than being alone and vulnerable like this.

My plan to render myself invisible didn't always work, however. When we passed a group of Russian POWs who were being taken the other direction down the road, one of them broke ranks and ran over to me. None of the German soldiers got riled; they just watched as he came and shook my hand.

"The best I can do," he said before joining his fellow prisoners and the confused-looking guards.

My hand smarted where he'd grabbed me, reminding me that though the shrapnel wound on my finger was small, it was far from healed. In my hand the soldier had placed a heel from a loaf of black bread.

We walked for two days, stopping occasionally to eat. Just as with the first squad, I was given the job of washing up after the meals and cleaning any boots the soldiers dropped in front of me. I didn't mind much. The soldiers ignored me most of the time, and if it weren't for the fact that there was always a soldier walking behind me with his gun trained on me, I might have been out on a training maneuver back at home.

We passed through village after village, town after town.
I flinched at every engine I heard, whether it was in the air
or on the ground, and at times the uncertainty threatened
to undo me. I had gotten through the war by following
orders and relying on the other men in my squad. Now I
was alone and vulnerable. It took everything I had to resist
giving in to fear.

On my third morning with the new squad, we were in a
heavily wooded area, still marching east. A twist in the track
revealed a dark building, hundreds of years old and at least
five stories high. It looked like a cross between a church and
a fairy-tale castle. We stopped there, and I was taken through
the front gate to the courtyard, where I was handed over
to another soldier and led up a narrow flight of stairs to a
dimly lit corridor. Heavy doors lined the passageway, and I
was shown into a small room. Bars covered the window and
the small viewing hole in the door, which had been shut and
locked behind me. There was a bunk bed along the wall, but
otherwise there was nothing else in the room.

I lay down on one of the dingy beds. The thin mattress,
though dry, smelled of urine, but I was too tired to care.

In the few minutes before sleep overtook me, I thought
of Betty. She seemed so far away right now, and I wondered
whether I would ever see her again.

The door opened, and a short, tired-looking man
stumbled in.

"Hello," I said.

He said something I couldn't understand.

"American," I said, pointing at my chest.

"Turkish," he said flatly before climbing onto the bunk above me.

My thoughts returned to Betty and how much I wanted to get out of all this and marry her. I thought about settling down back in Columbus or maybe in Betty's home of Portland. I'd find a job and we'd raise a family, and I couldn't think of anything better than that.

I felt myself starting to itch. I hadn't changed my uniform since before we crossed the Rhine, and that was weeks ago. By now I was used to the way the rough fabric felt against my skin, but this itching was something new. I scratched my chest and looked at my fingers to find a dead flea between them. Soon there was another itch, and I pulled off another flea. I was sure I saw one jump from the upper mattress onto me.

The door opened, and I was led away—though plenty of the fleas came with me. I headed down the stairs and out into the courtyard, where I was taken to a waiting cart with a shaggy-looking horse attached to the front. An old man on the driver's bench motioned for me to climb in behind him, and as soon as I sat down I was joined by a second guard. Clearly escape wasn't going to be an option.

"Are you scared?" he asked.

"No," I lied.

"Well, don't be. We're going to take you near Munich, then you'll walk the rest of the way."

I appreciated his efforts to reassure me, but the news did little to change the sense of uncertainty that was clinging to me like the sweat and grime that had been my constant companions since I'd landed in France the previous year. Still, I tried to sit back and let the journey unfold.

To my surprise, I was able to enjoy the beauty of the countryside. We passed steep hills thick with fir and pine trees, wide-open meadows, and clear lakes that reflected the blue sky. I inhaled deeply, taking in the cleanest air I'd breathed since leaving home.

Munich was farther than I thought, and we traveled the rest of the day with nothing other than the sound of the horse's hooves to break the silence. It was strangely tranquil, and I was grateful for every mile I didn't have to walk.

Our journey ended when we reached yet another town, where I was passed on to another group of German soldiers. They appeared different from the others—colder somehow, less predictable. It was hard to say why I felt this way, but something about their demeanor led me to doubt whether they'd resist an order from an SS officer to turn me in.

The walk to Munich took a full twenty-four hours. We passed factories and large units of troops, and German tanks lined the side of the road. We must have passed hundreds of German troops, and I couldn't believe none of them were SS. But I kept my head down and didn't dare to look up to see precisely whom we were passing.

Eventually, once the road was flanked by tall buildings that blocked out the mountains beyond, we approached our destination. It was another prison, but this one looked different. It was large and squat, and where the previous prison had a touch of whimsy about it, this one was so stark and austere that it seemed as if no sunlight had ever shone upon it.

I was taken inside to a low-ceilinged room. There were no bunks, and the twenty or thirty men inside had grouped themselves by nationality. I spotted a couple of GIs near the door and walked up to them.

"I'm glad to see you," I said, experiencing a wash of relief.

They said hello and nodded at me with half smiles.

I sat down on the floor next to them. "How long do you think we'll be here?"

"How long?" The speaker seemed to be the younger of the two. "The two of us are supposed to get shot in the morning."

All at once I felt cold and desperately tired. I'd ended up in the wrong place again. Would God get me out of here?

"Where did you escape from?" the soldier asked me.

"Escape?" I said. "No, I just got caught a few days ago. They said they were taking me to a POW camp."

Both GIs looked doubtful.

"This is not a POW camp," the older one said.

"Everyone here is an escapee. The Krauts hate people breaking out. The only reason they recapture them is so they can kill them. That's why we're all here."

I thought about what he said. Could it be that the Germans thought I was an escapee? My initial captors knew I wasn't—they'd found me with my rations and rifle and helmet—but what about all the other groups that had escorted me to Munich? I hadn't seen any papers change hands as I was passed along, and no one had asked me any questions since the night outside the barn. If everyone else was in here because they'd been caught escaping, what were the chances that any of the Germans here would believe me?

There wasn't much more to say after that. I sat back and tried to think. I felt in my breast pocket for my Bible, even though I knew it wasn't there. I wanted to hold it, to smell it, to gain some ounce of comfort from it. If this was going to be my last night alive—or, if I was lucky, my last week alive—I wanted something that would help me cling to God.

I thought back to the stories and verses that had seen me through thus far. The challenge given to Joshua resonated loudly within me. I repeated the words to myself, willing them to be true: *Be strong and of a good courage; be not afraid, neither be thou dismayed.*

It wasn't easy. For all my attempts to remember the words and recite them to myself, I felt the urge to panic. I kept running through my situation, like a riddle I hoped I could solve. But no matter how many times I went through it, I always came to the same conclusion: at some point, someone must have decided I was a former prisoner. And with the war so close to being over and the Germans in full retreat, there really was only one thing to do with prisoners.

The same scenario played in my mind time after time: me standing blindfolded, with my hands tied behind my back, my fingers touching a wall that was sprayed with bullet holes. In front of me I heard the sound of guns loading and a man giving the order to take aim.

The images burrowed into my mind like the fleas that were gnawing at my flesh. I tried to scratch them out, but neither the fleas nor the images of my death were easy to get rid of. Both had a tight grip on me and wouldn't let go.

My mind was racing with horrific thoughts, my body was itching and aching all over, and my soul felt heavy. I was so locked in my own private battles that I wasn't aware of anything or anyone else in the room.

For the Lord thy God is with thee whithersoever thou goest.

The words came to me, and I reached for them the way a drowning man reaches for a branch.

Whithersoever thou goest.

Wherever I was, God would be with me. I thought back to the SS officer in the sidecar and the sergeant who had disobeyed his orders. God had been with me then—I knew it. I remembered the first officer who had approached me with his knife. God had protected me then, too. Then there was the shell that should have killed me but failed

to explode. I knew there were dozens of other times too—
moments when men right next to me had died from bullet
wounds—and times when I'd run from a position that,
seconds later, was turned into a cloud of earth and smoke
and shrapnel.

And then there was the time I'd looked up from my
hospital bed to see Betty walk over to me and ask me if I
was a Christian.

The Lord thy God is with thee whithersoever thou goest.

The fear didn't leave me as I traced God's faithfulness in
the past, but at least it stopped consuming me. The more
I remembered what God had done, the easier it became to
pray. I thanked God for rescuing me and for steering me on
this journey—the one that had ended up so different from
my earliest plans, when I was going to be a pilot.

I knelt down to pray, and as I did, the pain in my leg,
the itching beneath my skin, and the thirst that cracked my
throat faded a little. I thanked God and begged Him for
yet more help.

"I'm in the wrong place again, Lord!" I said. "But I know
You are with me here, too."

167th General Hospital
Cherbourg, France

April 15, 1945

Dearest Ray,

The most horrible thing happened today at mail call. Major Leonard came to my tent and called my name. She looked different than she normally does—kind of sad and concerned. My first thought was that she had found out about us. I was afraid she was going to tell me that I would be disciplined for fraternizing with you and that she was sending me far, far away. But it was so much worse than that. She just handed me two letters and walked out. They were the last letters I wrote to you. Across the address of each was a stamp. One read KILLED IN ACTION. RETURN TO SENDER; the other MISSING IN ACTION. RETURN TO SENDER.

Oh, Ray, I don't even know what to think. The girls have been trying to comfort me, telling me stories about how this has happened before and the soldier wasn't really dead after all. They say that there are all kinds of possible explanations and that I shouldn't give up hope.

I don't want to give up hope. But all day I've felt like there is a weight inside me, and it's a terrifying feeling. My mind keeps taunting me with different thoughts of what might have happened to you. Just when I flush one of them away, another one creeps in.

I remember the old Bible story of Jacob wrestling with the angel. That's what I'm doing. I'm holding on to the hope that I have in God. I believe that God brought us together, and I don't believe He did that so it would end like this.

So I am praying for you. With every breath that leaves my body, I am praying for you. I am praying that you are alive, that you just went missing or something, and that soon you will get these words and hold this letter in your hands.

The girls say I should tell you my news—that if you're
reading this in a foxhole somewhere, you'll want to hear
about more than my worries and fears. So the news is that
we finally got our wool underwear! After the coldest winter
imaginable, we finally got them. Not that we have much use
for them now. The snow is long gone, and flowers are starting
to come out in little clusters. It's almost pretty at times.

There's a rumor going around that the actress Dorothy
McGuire might be visiting France sometime soon. I don't
know if I believe it or not, but it's funny how even just a little
hint of Hollywood gets everyone all excited.

I remember going to the movies with you while you were
here. They keep playing that same Bing Crosby picture,
and it reminds me of your story about how you hoped to see
him when you were at Gonzaga. Isn't it amazing to think
that I was at Fort George Wright in Spokane too? I never
saw him either, but I love thinking that we share some of the
same past.

If I ever want to smile, all I have to do is think about the
times we spent walking to church or to the movies together.
Do you remember how we counted how many warts we
had on our hands and compared notes? It wasn't exactly
romantic, was it? But the girls tell me that love comes in all
shapes and sizes, and that there's more to romance than
flowers and sunsets.

What I know for sure is this: from the moment we met
and started talking, I felt that God was at work. As the days
passed and we spent more and more time together, I became
convinced that these strange journeys we've both been on—
your dropping out of the Navy Air Corps and my getting
turned down by the Navy—are the result of God's mighty
work. But for God, you might have been a pilot and I might
have been a nurse on a ship in the Pacific. But for God, I
don't think we would have met. But for God, I would not be
writing to you today.

I believe you're alive, Ray. I believe we're going to meet again. And when we do, I'll take the ring you gave me off the chain where it sits with my dog tags and put it on my finger. We'll find a minister and some friends to stand up with us, and we'll get married. And after that, Ray and Betty Whipps will begin the adventure of a whole new life together.

I pray that as you read these words, you'll believe it with me, Ray.

I love you.
Betty

16

LIFE BY A THREAD

AT FIRST IT SOUNDED LIKE THE WIND, as if a wild storm were preparing to strike just beyond the walls of the air-raid shelter. The sound was masked slightly by the wail of the sirens, but it was there all right. And with every second that passed, the sound grew louder. It wouldn't be long now: the bombers were almost here.

I looked around me. We were packed in tight around the air-raid shelter, each man sitting with his legs folded up in front of him. Some looked around anxiously; others just looked tired, their heads hanging low. Nobody talked.

Just twenty minutes earlier, we were all in the low-ceilinged cell where I'd met the GIs. I'd been praying ever since I heard they expected to be executed in the morning, pleading with God to intervene and save us all. I hadn't noticed the heavy door open, but I looked up when the room went silent. A handful of German soldiers were walking into the room, holding their rifles across their chests. Judging by the nervous looks that were being passed from prisoner to prisoner, nothing like this had happened before. Or if it had, things hadn't ended well when it did.

All of us prisoners were herded out of the room, into the darkness that hung over the yard. The soldiers hurried us across the stones and down a narrow set of stairs that led beneath a metal-roofed building. As I took the first steps, the sirens began to blare, filling the air with their high-pitched wails. Suddenly hurrying seemed like a good idea after all.

The guards joined us and sat at each end of the shelter, their weapons at the ready. We all sat in silence, waiting.

In time it became clear that this wasn't a single bomber approaching the city, but four or five of them. The deep hum and throb of the engines grew louder and louder, and a whisper was going around among the men that they were American B-17s. I could feel the ground begin to shake.

When the bombs first started, they were far enough away that we could still hear the sirens. But soon the bombs were getting closer and louder, until eventually the explosions were the only thing we could hear. It was obvious that at least part of the attack was targeted on the prison just outside these doors. Even though the shelter must have been the safest place in the prison, it felt exposed and unprotected. My prayers split off in two different directions as I thanked God for destroying the prison but pleaded with Him to spare the lives of the men around me.

At last the bombs and sirens stopped. The soldiers guarding us bustled us toward the door, shouting, "Everybody out!"

Once we got outside, we saw that a whole wing of the prison had been destroyed and there were fires burning all around. The windows had been blown open and the ground was now covered in debris. Men ran frantically in and out of the prison, and I could hear voices shouting from inside.

If the Germans who were guarding us were bothered by any of this, they didn't show it. Instead, they had us line up and stand in silence. I could still hear the echo of my prayers within my head: *Please God, if it's Your will, help me make it through this.*

For the longest time we just stood there. Not a single person dared to talk. We simply waited and watched, wondering what on earth the Germans were going to do with us. It was clear that the bombing of the prison had thrown their plans into chaos, and between the long periods of silence when the soldiers just watched us, they talked anxiously among themselves.

"They could kill us all right now," a British voice whispered behind me. I didn't dare to turn around and look. I just listened as others joined in the hushed discussion.

"They wouldn't do that." This voice had an accent I didn't recognize.

"You think not?" the Brit said. "What else do you think they're going to do with us? Besides, wouldn't you want revenge for all this bombing?"

A painful silence settled on us.

After we'd stood outside for several hours, an officer directed his soldiers to put us in groups of five or six. Then he told us that we should be ready to march. "We're taking you to a prisoner-of-war camp."

I wasn't sure what to expect at our next destination, but I was relieved to leave behind the rubble and smoke of the prison. It was a long walk, and as the hours passed and the night gave way to day, I realized how tired I was. I'd started the war in the best shape of my life, easily able to tackle any obstacle course the Army or Navy threw at me. It was that fitness that was partly responsible for my surviving as long as I did.

But after just a few days of being a prisoner, my body was beginning to show the strain. Not only was the wound I'd received on my finger looking nasty—it was giving off heat and looking swollen and angry—but even a short march was enough to leave me struggling for breath. Whenever I moved I felt tired, and whenever I stopped I wanted to sleep.

The farther we walked, the worse I felt. Between my filthy uniform and my filthy skin, my flesh was suffocating, and every few yards I felt heavier and slower. I didn't take in the scenery around me, and I didn't even think of finding a way to escape. All I could do was drag one weary leg after the other, hoping with every step that it would be over soon.

✪

It took most of the day, but eventually the boots in front of me came to a stop, and I looked up. A wooden guard tower rose above us, standing tall and stark on the horizon. Low wooden huts lined the approach to the tower, and soldiers shouted at us to move forward and separate ourselves by nationality. I looked for the two GIs but couldn't see them anywhere.

Nobody had spoken a word while we marched out of Munich, but now a new kind of silence fell on us as we entered the camp. We passed beneath the guard tower and through a tall gate, and I wondered whether I would ever get out again.

Up until now, I'd become familiar with a certain type of fear—the type that accompanied 88s and gunfire and subjected my body to grand surges of adrenaline. I'd experienced this feeling so many times that, while it never got easier or less intense, when the battles started up my body knew what to do. I'd felt the same fear as I prayed on my knees in Munich and when I was hauled into the cold night air by the knife-wielding German soldier. Danger was close, and I needed to keep alert.

But as I walked into the camp, I felt different. For

months I'd known that my boots, my eyes, my hands, and my legs were the tools that would ensure my survival. If I was quick, alert, and strong enough, I'd stand a chance of making it. But not in here. No instinct kicked in telling me to run or fight or become acutely aware of what was going on around me; instead, I simply felt overwhelmed. It was as if the air in the camp had somehow been stripped of half its oxygen, leaving me feeling suffocated. For the first time since June 1944, I started to doubt whether I could trust my body to get me out of there.

Stalag VII-A was a giant camp—a whole city made of timber and razor wire. It was so vast that those men trapped inside seemed like ants. Within its confines, I suddenly felt insignificant, powerless, and weak. It was impossible to tell how many thousands of Allied troops were imprisoned there, but I'd never seen so many soldiers gathered in one place—not when we left Camp Kilmer, not when we arrived in Liverpool, and not even when we landed in Normandy. And yet here we all were, a whole army's worth of troops, penned up like cattle. We were a sorry bunch.

For the last few weeks I'd been in battle, the only time I'd encountered German soldiers was when they were in retreat, and it was easy to believe the war would soon be over. All that optimism and confidence evaporated as soon as I reached Stalag VII-A. The Germans showed no sign of retreating or giving up. For the first time, I entertained the thought that our victory might not be quite so inevitable after all.

But there was something else that troubled me as I pushed my way through the crowds of people lining the muddy tracks between the wooden huts. As I studied the faces of the men I passed, I wasn't sure I'd make it out of this place alive. It was as if the very air in Stalag VII-A was incapable of sustaining life. The men I passed looked tired, thin, and weak—and worst of all, defeated. Many of them were clearly ill, and with their sunken cheeks and hollow eyes, they seemed to be shadows of the soldiers they'd once been. To me, it was instantly clear that this was a place where life was slowly suffocated.

We were marched forward, passing row upon row of wooden huts that lay on either side of a network of straight paths. The camp was divided by barbed-wire fencing into different yards. Minutes passed as we kept walking, and I still had no clearer idea of where the camp ended. Allied soldiers were everywhere, staring with the same vacant expression. They were packed in tight, sitting in doorways, crowding around windows, pushing alongside one another as they stood around outside. For all their number, few of them bothered to look up as we squeezed past. With every step, my hope continued to fade. I was walking among ghosts. Soon I would be one of them.

Along with the mass of people, there was another constant that was almost impossible to escape. All around the perimeter of the camp were wooden guard towers. Each one was topped with a pair of soldiers and a machine gun, and tall barbed-wire fences ran along the ground between them. Any thought of being able to escape left my mind.

A handful of other GIs and I were taken to a yard where the sleeping quarters were not huts but battered canvas tents. Each of them contained mats on the floor in place of bunks. Since I was the last one in, I took the only mat available, the one by the door. It reminded me of being back in the tent at Betty's hospital, but I was too weary and worried to know whether to be comforted or saddened by that. So I lay down, closed my eyes, and tried desperately to remember the moment I first saw Betty. It was no good. All I could think about was the empty doorway near me and the cold void waiting on the other side.

The days started early at Stalag VII-A. We were awakened by the sound of a soldier shouting, calling us to line up for roll call. His orders were followed by the noise of fifty weary men in the tent, all getting up and shuffling their way through the doorway next to me. I joined them, not knowing what was happening, but relieved that none of them looked panicked or surprised by what was going on. I guessed it was around five o'clock in the morning, because the first traces of light were sitting low in the sky as we lined up outside.

The cold air bit into my bones, but there were other aches too. My back felt rusty and sore all the way down, the wound on my finger was raging, and my head was crawling with lice. I hadn't slept well; a knot of worry had prevented me from falling into a deep sleep. For most of the night I'd stared at the tent doorway and watched as the breeze blew it open and closed.

"Don't worry," a voice beside me whispered.

We were standing in lines five men wide. I startled a bit—it was the first time someone other than a guard had spoken to me since I arrived at Stalag VII-A. I glanced up to see a man looking at me with a smile a mile wide that looked completely out of place in the camp.

"They've almost given up on us," he said. "All we have to do is keep quiet and dig in. It'll all be over soon."

He was unlike any of the men I'd seen on my way in. Though he looked thin and weak, he was no ghost.

Even though I wanted to believe him, I wasn't sure I could. It had taken only a night, but already I felt like I had lost too much of the battle.

We stood that way for almost an hour, silently staring at the ground. Eventually a German soldier came and took roll. When he was satisfied that everybody was accounted for, he dismissed us and motioned for us to eat. I joined the long line that ended at a metal barrel standing on its end. There was a gentle heat coming from underneath it, but what I saw inside was a lot less inviting. It looked like nothing more than water, flies, and assorted weeds—the kind of fake stew a child might make for fun in the backyard. The man serving noticed me hesitating, but he just stared blankly and handed over a small metal canteen half full of the liquid. I tried not to think of what was in it as I found a place to sit.

"The name's George Stall," the man with the brilliant smile said. "The food's a whole lot worse than it used to be."

"How come?"

"They used to give us bologna and bread, and this soup used to have potatoes in it instead of weeds and flies, but that was when they could feed themselves. Now the Germans live off our Red Cross rations." He looked at my tin. "We're just trying to survive on this."

After another pause, he said softly, "Not everyone makes it."

George told me that the camp was full of tens of thousands of Allied prisoners. "Most days they send us out to work detail, repairing the railroads or clearing up the towns after a bombing. It's not bad out there, and it's better than being bored in here."

That first day in Stalag VII-A wasn't a work day for us, and as the hours crept by, I discovered how right George was about boredom. Time moved slowly, and as the day stretched on I began to feel worse. My finger was now so painful that I didn't want to pick anything up with my right hand. I worried how I'd cope with working on a railroad.

Spending time with George that day was the only thing that helped to lift the gloom that had descended since I'd arrived. It had been too long since I'd been able to sit and talk freely to someone without fearing an imminent attack or a sudden order to move out. George's story was interesting, and so different from mine. Like me, he was from Columbus, but he was a paratrooper instead of an infantryman. He'd been captured ten months earlier, after he'd parachuted into Holland. Everyone else in his platoon was either killed or captured, and though he looked thin, he wasn't emaciated. His broad smile came easily, especially when he spoke about his wife.

"I miss Fran," he told me. "But it's easier now that I know I'll be seeing her soon."

George's optimism was appealing, but it wasn't enough to dispel my fear. I was feeling sick, and my finger was getting worse. I'd kept my hand in my pocket most of the day, partly in an attempt to protect it from getting jostled and partly because I didn't like the feeling I got whenever I looked at it.

The throbbing wouldn't go away, and late in the afternoon I eased it out of my pocket to take a look. The whole finger was swollen and red, and the place where the shrapnel had embedded itself in my skin was now open and oozing. Little yellow pillows surrounded the wound, and the whole thing emitted a smell that made me wince. Even worse, the pain was starting to spread to my other fingers too.

"That does not look good," George said. "You need to get that looked at."

I shrugged.

"Come on, I'll take you to see Louis."

I followed him through an open gate at the end of our yard.

"They used to keep us separated all the time," he said, "but lately they've taken in so many new prisoners that they don't bother much. Just as long as we're all in the right places in the morning for roll call."

George marched quickly down lanes, stepping over people as he went. With every corner we turned and every avenue we crossed, I realized again how big the camp was. When I arrived, I'd assumed it held a thousand or so, but after walking for five minutes and still seeing endless rows of huts, it struck me that there might have been fifty times that number. This wasn't a camp; it was a city.

We turned a final corner and stopped outside a hut where a group of Frenchmen were sitting.

"Ah, Jorge!" said a neat-looking Frenchman with dark hair and even darker eyes. "How are you?"

"Louis," George said. "I'm fine. But my friend Ray here isn't doing so good." He nudged me forward and had me hold out my hand.

Louis looked at it carefully, holding his face close as if he were inspecting a painting.

"This is not good." He pulled me inside the hut and had me sit down near a stove. I watched as he filled a small can with water and heated it up. "How did it happen?" he asked.

I told him about the strafing and diving under the truck and how I didn't know whether it was glass or shrapnel.

"Hmm. It is now infected. That is *le problème*, huh?"

I watched as the water turned cloudy and the first thin wisps of steam started to rise from it. He dabbed his finger into the near-boiling water. "You are ready, Raimon?"

I nodded, not quite sure what I was agreeing to.

"Then give me your hand."

He lifted the can from the stove and placed it on the ground. Grabbing my right hand, he pushed my thumb back and plunged my first two fingers into the water. The pain raced up my arm and across my chest, as if someone were dragging a knife across my flesh. I pulled as hard as I could, but Louis's two-handed grip was firm. I closed my eyes and tried to think of something else, but the only thing in my mind was pain, pure pain.

Finally Louis let go. I pulled my hand free and felt a fresh wave of pain explode in my finger. I felt tears on my face and realized I must have been crying.

Louis looked at me with a kind smile. "You need to come back tomorrow, Raimon. It is the only way to fix this."

George took me back to my tent, though we walked slower this time. Another night of fitful sleep and constant itching followed, this time accompanied by occasional gusts of wind that blew the rain in through the half-open tent flaps. By the time the German shouts for us to get up broke the silence, I was desperate to get away from my infested mat. I stood with the others, my clothes getting wetter and heavier, and waited for roll call to commence. I glanced at the metal drum and saw the same collection of weeds, flies, and water and decided to ask George to show me how to get to Louis instead.

The pain was no less than the day before, but the antici-pation was worse. Louis had to pull a little harder to get my hand into the can, and though I knew it was going to help, I found myself resisting as the scalding water bit into my flesh. Still, the relief was all the sweeter once it was over. When Louis told me he would see me again that evening, I agreed and tried to put the appointment out of my mind.

That day it was our turn to work outside the camp. We were loaded onto trucks and taken a few miles away, where we were told to clean up the wreckage from a bomb explosion in the middle of a town. It must have happened several days before, since I didn't see any wounded people in the area.

George was in an even better mood than usual. As we worked side by side, he made comments under his breath about how the war was sure to be over soon and how much he was looking forward to seeing his wife, Fran, when he got home.

He was climbing some steps nearby to pick up rubble, when he started whistling. Out of the corner of my eye, I noticed a soldier rush into view, his rifle raised high. As George was bending down to pick up bricks, whistling all the while, the soldier brought the butt of his rifle down hard at the base of his neck. There was a mighty crack, and George crumpled to the ground as if all the life had been instantly drained from him. The German turned and walked away, shooting a glare at me as he went.

I ran over to George, who was struggling to his knees.

"I'm okay," he said, brushing me away. "We need to keep working."

He struggled the rest of the day. It was obvious that every stone he lifted caused him pain, and his typical smile was nowhere to be seen. The day seemed darker and bleaker without his usual happy countenance.

We got back to the camp late that night, but I still made time to visit Louis and get my finger treated. The pain was just as fierce, but this time I remembered George and how he'd been knocked down but refused to be defeated by it.

"Those Germans are dangerous," I told Louis when he asked where George was. "George thinks the war will be over soon, but I'm not so sure. They seem pretty desperate."

"Ah, Raimon. Maybe Jorge is right. Maybe the war is ending very soon." With that, he smiled mischievously and patted me on the shoulder. "All you must do is stay alive, yes? You need to eat, even if it is just that water they are serving."

I went back to my tent and thought about what he'd said. He seemed confident, but not in an optimistic way—more like he knew something. It gave me hope.

The rest of my first week in Stalag VII-A was more of the same. I visited Louis for my twice-daily pain sessions, tried to look anonymous and unthreatening whenever I was anywhere near a German soldier, and even managed to force down some of what passed for food in those metal barrels. While my finger showed signs of recovery, the fleas and lice robbed me of most of my sleep and the constant hunger left me weak.

My body was running on reserves, and at this rate I wasn't sure how long I could last. Certainly the idea of making it through to the summer felt impossible. When I mentioned this to Louis, he suggested I give up sleeping in my tent and spend each night in the hut with the Frenchmen instead.

"We have fleas just the same, Raimon," he said. "But at least you will be dry."

I gladly took him up on his offer.

More than anything, I sensed how weak and overwhelmed I was. I looked at men like Louis and George, who had managed to get this far without looking like skeletons. How did they do it? For every man who looked reasonably well like them, there were a hundred other men who didn't. The odds were clearly against me. Perhaps if I'd arrived feeling strong and healthy, things might have been different. But I was weak and sick and on the brink of exhaustion.

"You've got to trade," George said one day. "Buy yourself some food when you're out of the camp on work detail."

"With what? I don't have any money."

"Just wait," he said.

He was right. A few days later, we came back from work detail in the early evening to find an unusual hum of noise and excitement in the camp. Red Cross parcels had been delivered and were being distributed among the men in my tent. Like every other man, I received a box large enough to hold a pair of shoes that contained just two cigarettes and a bar of chocolate. The chocolate was the best thing that had crossed my lips since I was a kid eating out of my mother's and Goffie's kitchens. It sent a warm feeling through me as I savored each square throughout the evening. The cigarettes were less exciting, but George quickly put me straight.

"Now you've got something you can trade with. You'd be surprised what someone will give you for a Lucky."

"Aren't we supposed to get more than this from the Red Cross parcels?"

"Yeah. The Germans have been taking everything but the chocolate and cigarettes for months—all the cheese, meat, and coffee. Plus, we're supposed to get one parcel a week, but that's never happened."

The next day we were taken to the outskirts of another large town, where we had to clear rubble again. When I saw that it was clear, I motioned to an older man who was passing by.

"Zigaretten?" I said, holding one out to him while patting my stomach.

He knew exactly what I meant and was happy to trade two potatoes for one Lucky. It was a good deal for me, and I went to sleep that night feeling just a little less empty.

The same thing happened again when, a few days later, a woman offered me a bag of strange-looking seeds in return for my one remaining cigarette. Louis explained that they were not seeds but lentils and told me I could boil them and spread them out over a few days.

Though I felt I'd made good use of my currency, two potatoes, a few pounds of lentils, and two daily servings of watery soup wouldn't be enough to keep a grown man alive for long. And the work we were doing was using up even more energy—energy I didn't have.

As I ended my second week in Stalag VII-A, my finger was gradually getting better. It was no longer swollen and pussy—it was now just red and sore. Meanwhile, however, the rest of my body was showing signs of distress. My skin had broken out in pimples, clumps of hair were falling out whenever I tried to scratch away the lice, and my belly was starting to swell with the telltale indicator of malnutrition. I wasn't alone. Men were dying in the camp around me, and we all knew it. We just tried not to think about it.

Sleeping in the French hut had one major advantage. I finally discovered how Louis was so confident about the war's ending. On the first night I was with them, once it was dark and the guards had retreated to their wooden towers and their higher-quality huts, one of the Frenchmen pried up a floorboard under his bed and produced a radio.

"You see," Louis said, grinning by the half light of the stove as his friend tuned the radio, "we know *exactement* how the war is going."

Listening to the BBC that night was bittersweet. Hearing of the death of President Roosevelt was a blow

I hadn't expected. It had been his voice that I'd heard
on the radio back in Columbus, telling us that America
was at war; his voice that had brought my family—and
the whole nation—together in prayer. Yet along with the
sorrow I felt, I was excited to hear those English accents
describe the power of the Allies and the weakness of the
German forces.

By the time I entered my third week in Stalag VII-A,
I started to seriously fear that I wouldn't make it. Even
though the battles and foxholes and 88s were far away,
each day brought a new battle within me. I fought for
the energy to get back to the yard and stand upright with
my fellow Americans during roll call. I fought the urge to
throw away whatever was spooned into my canteen from
the metal barrel. I fought the urge to sleep when there was
work to be done outside the camp, and I fought the urge to
give up hope when I awoke from dreams about food that
left my stomach creased in agony.

I missed my Bible so much in those days, and as often
as I daydreamed about eating a pound of cooked bacon, I
also pictured myself sitting alone, healthy and safe, reading
Scripture. But when these dreams were over, the suffocating
feelings returned. The only thing I could do was pray. I asked
God to be with me, to keep me safe, and to see me through.

"You've brought me this far," I'd whisper with wheezing
breaths. "Please don't let it end like this."

One morning it was harder than usual to move. I was tired and weak, but the problem was as much internal as external. Doubt and fear were crushing me. I had become like a drowning man who knows he's losing the energy to keep himself afloat. I stayed on the floor in Louis's hut and let myself drift.

For the first time since I arrived in the camp, I decided to write to Betty. It didn't matter that the soldiers had taken everything from me—including her address—or that I didn't have a pencil or paper. Even if I'd been able to find something to write with, there was no way a guard was going to mail a letter for me. But there was one thing they couldn't take away from me: my thoughts. So in my mind, I wrote a letter to Betty anyway.

Dearest Betty,

I wish I could write to you under different circumstances. I wish I were back home, preparing to come and meet your folks or have you be introduced to mine. I wish I could show you around Columbus, pointing out the trees I'd climbed as a boy and the river we swam in every summer. I wish I were sitting on the banks with you now, talking about life and the future and what our family would be like.

I wish I had better news for you, but the truth is that I'm holding on by my fingernails here. I'm not sure how much longer I can last.

All I really want to say is that I love you and that
I am still so thankful to God that we met.

And I hope we do again.

Your loving fiancé,

Ray

When the end finally came—the end of my war, not
the war—it was swift and surprising. I was so intent on
keeping myself alive that I didn't notice the number of
German guards dropping rapidly through the final week of
April. But late in the evening on Saturday, April 29, 1945,
we got word that all the German guards had gone.

I followed the rest of the men in Louis's hut outside.
We looked up at the guard towers and saw that, for the
first time since anyone could remember, they were empty.
I don't know if anyone tried to escape that night, or if you
could call walking out of an unmanned camp an escape,
but I knew all I could do was go back to my patch of dry
ground and sleep. If I could just wake up the next day,
I would be okay.

It was eerie not to have the guards around in the
morning. There was no need to stand in neat lines of five
and no need to keep quiet and subdued, in fear of incur-
ring a beating. Still, we stood around the yards, watching
and waiting. Mostly we just waited.

Finally, on the morning of Sunday, April 30, we heard
it: the low roar of heavy engines. But these were not the

angry sounds of German Panthers and Tigers or the noise of Allied bombers preparing to strike. They were the warm tones of American Stuarts and Shermans, Locusts and Grants. Some men cheered; others rushed to be the first to see our liberators as they came into view on their tanks.

I just sat outside the hut and listened as the sound of freedom grew louder and louder in my ears.

17

WOULD SHE SAY YES?

"Hey, Raimon, give it to 'em!"

I looked up to see the familiar face of Louis, grinning and waving from a knoll nearby. I waved back, smiling too. I'd almost finished taking the evening roll call, and as soon as it was done, I made my way over to see him.

"I'm going now," he said as I approached. "I wanted to say goodbye and give you this." He handed over a picture of himself. On the back he'd written his name and a few words in French that I couldn't quite translate. There would be time enough to do that when I got home.

"Thank you, Louis," I said. "Thank you so much."

We embraced. "Très bien, Raimon. Au revoir."

As he turned and walked away, I realized how little I knew about him. The note on the back of his photo told me his surname—Kaspar—but apart from that, I knew nothing. Was he married? Where was he going back to? What would life be like for him now in a country that had finally been freed from German occupation?

Though we were liberated on Sunday morning, we had to spend a couple of additional days around the camp. The French, Belgians, and everyone else who could make their own way home were allowed to do so, but the Americans and the Russians had to wait a few days in the camp until arrangements could be made to get us home. On Tuesday, the men in my original yard were finally loaded onto trucks and taken to a nearby airstrip, where we were told that a C3 plane would be taking us to Camp Lucky Strike in Le Havre, France. After that we'd be put on the first ship and sent back to Camp Kilmer, New Jersey. I wasn't sure where my friend George was headed, but I hoped we'd see each other again.

All the details made my head swim a little, but I didn't mind. With some decent K rations inside me, I was beginning to feel a little stronger. As I stood among the crowd of other GIs, I lazily scanned the skies for the C3's arrival.

A plane came into view, but it was far too small to be one of our transporters. The closer it came, the quieter the crowd became. It was clearly a fighter plane, but something about it looked out of place.

At last the Navy Air Corps officer who was waiting to give us the all clear to board spoke up. "It's a Messerschmitt."

We watched as it came close enough to reveal its markings. As it prepared to land, the plane started rocking its wings from side to side, as if caught up in high winds.

"Are we going to shoot it down?" one of our men asked.

"No," the officer told us. "He's surrendering."

It was as if all of us were suddenly struck with the same high-voltage thought. We strained to get a better view, watching the plane land safely.

"Easy, fellas," said the officer. "Not until he's stopped."

The pilot could have taxied and stopped anywhere, but he came to within twenty yards of where we were standing. We heard the engine cut, saw the propellers die, and watched as a tall, elegant pilot in full-dress uniform climbed out of the cockpit and dropped down to the ground below.

"Okay, boys." The officer stepped aside.

There must have been at least ten of us in the race to the pilot. It was a desperate sprint, and I surprised myself by how fast I was. I was sure that I'd been faster before wounding my leg and being starved for a month, but even so, I was the second person to reach him.

The first soldier to arrive, of course, took the Luger. I'd never wanted one anyway, so I wasn't disappointed to miss out on the firearm. Then, as I watched the German unbuckling the pistol and carefully handing it over, I saw the souvenir that I wanted: a dress sword, about a yard long, packed into a thin, black scabbard. I had come through the war—I'd made it out alive, escaping death more than once. What better trophy to show my future grandchildren than this?

When the German saw my gaze, he unfastened the sword and handed it over with all the ceremony of a three-star general awarding a field commission.

"Danke," I said, unsheathing the sword. It was beautiful, its blade clean and bright. I went to test how sharp it was with my finger, when the German spoke.

"No," he said. "It has never been touched."

I carefully pushed it back into the scabbard and walked away.

Arriving at Camp Lucky Strike in Le Havre brought a new level of relief. Knowing we were going home just as soon as they could load us onto a ship was enough, and the waiting didn't bother us. We spent our days eating dark chicken meat in an attempt to replace some of the protein that had been absent from our diet, and we spent our nights talking of the lives we'd build when we got home.

In some ways, I didn't want to leave. Le Havre was half a day's drive from Cherbourg, and I knew that if I tried, there was a chance I might be able to see Betty. The thought of it was thrilling, and I let my mind imagine how sweet it would be to talk to her, to hold her hand, and to hear her laugh as she told me more about her life back in Portland.

But there were doubts in my mind as well. I wondered whether I would be able to find a way around the age-old problem of her being an officer and me being an enlisted man. Worse than my military status was my physical condition. Though I felt a little better inside, I was still covered in pimples, my hair was teeming with lice, and my belly was swollen. I looked ill, old, and weak. What were the chances that Betty would still want to marry a man who looked like this? We barely knew each other, and months had passed since we said goodbye. I was sure that seeing me like this would be a nasty shock.

So I decided to wait. I planned to go home, get myself fixed up, and return to full health before I met Betty again—hopefully when she returned home sometime shortly after I did.

Meanwhile, I tried to write to her. I started letter after letter but shredded each one before I finished the first paragraph. Somehow the words never looked right on the page. How could a piece of paper express everything I felt—how I'd been so afraid to lose her and how she'd been my reason to stay alive through getting captured and being in the prison camp and going through everything else I'd faced? How could a few words do justice to how much I loved her—and how afraid I was that I wasn't worthy of her love?

There was also the practical matter that I didn't have her address. I'd lost her APO number when the first German soldiers took all my possessions, including her letters. I could write to her at the 167th General Hospital and hope that someone would pass on the letter, but I figured this would only add to the evidence that I was a forgetful, broken man who was struggling to cope after the war. So I reasoned that it would be better to wait a week or so until I was home, then write properly, making sure she would get my letter. Officer or not, I wanted to prove that I was man enough for her.

After eight days in Le Havre, we boarded the ship that would take us home. Bunks were close together, and I knew that if I left my sword unattended for any length of time, it would be liberated by another souvenir hunter, so I spent the eight days it took to cross the Atlantic clutching my sword as if my life depended upon it.

The wounded and injured had been given priority on the first ships, being sent over before us former POWs who were well enough to walk aboard unaided. Even so, it was a little shocking to see how some of our men looked compared to the crew. Everyone had sunken jaws and prominent ribs, but some looked even worse. I marveled at them, wondering how much worse the men who had gone before must have looked.

The days on the boat were a blur of laughter and full bellies. We talked about the future ahead of us, and there were card games that never seemed to end. The nights, however, were a different story. When all the talking and laughing ceased and the sound of the ship's engines grew louder, other sounds emerged. Lying there in the dark, holding on to my sword, I heard men call out in their sleep.

"We've got to get up!" one guy near me shouted almost every night. "We've *got* to get up!"

And as I heard him plead, I pictured myself crouching in front of a German pillbox, calling on my men, urging them forward as bullets clapped overhead. Other men cried out from different dreams, some fighting off terror, others replaying some agonizing trauma. One night I woke to the sound of a man desperately trying to muffle his sobs with his pillow.

Nobody talked much about what we'd been through. That was just the way it was. But when our ship came to a pause in the waters south of Brooklyn, every single one of us stood on deck, united in our silence as we watched a tugboat prepare to haul us that last stretch toward home.

As we came through the Narrows and up the Hudson River, the silence grew heavier still. The little tug kept pulling us along, guiding us through to the end of our long journey.

Finally, as we came level with the Statue of Liberty, the crying started. Inside each of us, stoppered up like poison, were months and years of war, pain, and fear. We'd buried it in order to fight and survive, but as we drifted by Liberty Island, our cheeks wet and our breathing stalled, just a little of that pain and fear was released.

Two days later, with the late May afternoon drawing to a close, I turned left onto East Maynard Avenue in Columbus. I walked the length of the street, down toward the tall beech tree that hid the railroad lines beyond it. I knocked on the door of 493, put my duffel bag on the porch, and listened to the sound of footsteps charging

down the stairs. It had been almost a year since I'd left
for Europe, a year since I'd said goodbye to my mother
and father.

They both opened the door, and I fell into their arms.
None of us wanted to let go.

When the crying and laughing had subsided just a little
and we'd made our way inside, my mother broke away for a
second and disappeared into the kitchen.

"We just received a letter," she said, returning with an
envelope in her hand. She smiled as she handed it over to
me. "It's from Lieutenant Betty Carter. I think maybe she'd
prefer a reply from you over one from us, don't you?"

I read her letter. It wasn't long, and she didn't mention
our engagement, but her care for me was obvious. It was
hard for me to contain my excitement, and after a few
more tears and embraces, I rushed upstairs. With a pen
and pad of paper, I pulled a chair up to an old desk and
sat down to write the words that had been growing louder
within me ever since we'd said our last goodbye.

493 East Maynard Avenue
Columbus, Ohio

May 27, 1945

To my darling Betty,

I arrived home today. There was so much joy and so many tears, but nothing compared to how I felt when I was handed the letter you sent to my parents, asking if they had any news about me. To know that you are well and that you still care enough about me to write filled me from top to bottom with joy.

I am well. I was captured after we crossed into Germany and taken to a prisoner-of-war camp outside Munich. It was tough in there for a while, but thanks to the Lord, the hope of seeing you again, and the advancing Allied forces, I managed to hold on 'til the end.

I don't quite know what I'm going to do now that I'm home. There's talk of us POWs being taken down to Miami Beach for a week to recuperate some more, but what I really want to do is stay here, sleep, and just be still. After we were liberated, we were moved like cargo across France and finally shipped across the Atlantic. I've had enough of being a soldier for now. I just want to be as far away from it all as I can get.

After I was captured, I thought a lot about those thirty days we spent together in your hospital in Cherbourg. Even though I didn't know much about you, I was convinced God had brought us together for a purpose. That's why, even when things got as bad as they did for me, I felt there was still something to hope for. As long as I was alive, there was a chance you and I could see each other again. As long as I was still breathing, there was a chance that our story could have more pages yet to be written.

From that very first day when I saw you in the tent, I've been struck not only by how beautiful you are but also by the way you are able to touch others with your smile, your kindness, and your light.

Betty, I'm so thankful you wrote to ask about me. May I ask one thing of you in return? I'm a little beaten up and I don't look too good right now, even though every day I'm regaining strength.

Will you still marry me?

Your loving and willing fiancé,
Ray

Marseilles, France

August 23, 1945

To my dearest Ray,

You are alive! I can't begin to explain how great it is to be able to write those words. You are alive, Ray! You are alive! My heart is pounding and my whole body is shaking with excitement, and even though it has now been three hours since I discovered this wonderful, wonderful truth, I keep closing my eyes every few minutes and calling out my thanks to God.

Even the way your letter arrived is a sign of how much we can trust the Lord. You posted the letter in June, but it took nearly three months to reach me. The envelope had the wrong APO number on it—just one digit was wrong. (It was such a simple mistake, and after all you've been through, I'm amazed you can still write at all, let alone send me such beautiful words.) Your letter got stuck somewhere, I guess, but eventually someone in the mail room at the 167th must have worked it out, put the correct number on it, and sent it on to me. God bless that person, whoever they are!

I'm no longer in Cherbourg. After the Germans surrendered, we were told that we were going to be redeployed to the Pacific. They loaded us up onto "forty and eights" (just like the ones my dad traveled on when he served here in 1918), and we took the railroad all the way down to Marseilles. By the way, this city is nicer than Cherbourg. A whole lot nicer.

The weeks passed, and the plans for our departure kept on changing. At first they were waiting to send us through the Panama Canal, but reports kept coming back about whole ships full of people getting sick with malaria. They waited a little while longer, and until last week the plan was that we would sail back to America before flying to the Philippines. Then the Japanese surrendered and everything changed.

But still I had no idea if you were alive or dead. All I knew was that we were preparing to board a ship and sail home and that I would just have to sit out the journey and hope to find out something about what happened to you once I was back home. I wasn't looking forward to the journey at all. Even the joy of the war being over couldn't fully lift my spirits, and just yesterday I kept going over the possibilities in my mind—that you'd been captured and were slowly making your way home, that you'd been wounded and were still receiving treatment, that somehow you were fine but hadn't been able to write.

This morning I was praying that something would happen, begging God to let me know what had happened to you. I joined the other girls as we were taken to the port. They were all so excited to be going home, and I was pleased for them, but I found it hard to do anything more than slump down on my duffel bag and feel the sun getting hotter with every hour that passed.

And then, just an hour before we boarded, we had mail call—the very last mail call in France. In the months since you disappeared, I'd been through so many of these mail calls, and each time I felt pulled in opposite directions. Part of me was always hoping for some good news, but there was another part of me that dreaded the return of yet another letter stamped MIA or KIA across it, or worse. Sometimes it just felt easier not to get any mail at all.

But this time the officer called my name. I walked over and reached out my hand for the letter he was holding.

As soon as I saw your writing on the front, I knew you were alive. I let out the loudest, longest scream you've heard in your entire life! The whole dock must have heard me. Some of the girls came over to see what was happening, and between the laughter and the tears and my clutching your letter to my chest like it was a newborn baby, they worked it out soon enough.

It took me the longest time to calm down enough to read what you wrote, but when I did, fresh tears and shouts of delight filled the air around me. I can't find the words to explain my relief and joy. I want to keep screaming like I did on the dock!

I want you to know that I never doubted that you were alive. I worried that I was wrong, and I had to fight so hard to push back the sorrow that kept trying to take root inside me, but deep down I always knew I could trust God for you. I knew it because all along, trusting God is the only thing that's ever really helped to make sense of any of this. I've had to trust God for safety, trust Him for wisdom, and trust Him for us.

I write this knowing I won't be able to send it until we land back home. They hope we'll make it by Labor Day, and it would seem right if we did. All this work, all this struggle and sacrifice is now over, and it seems right to be back in time to celebrate.

It's also time for us to start our new life, our new adventure together. In reply to the final question in your letter, I say YES—a thousand times YES. I am honored to become your wife, and that day cannot come soon enough.

Your loving fiancée,
Betty

Epilogue

I CALL IT MY *GOOD WOUND*, because it was thanks to the piece of German shrapnel that tore my leg open that I met Betty. From that one injury came so many other good things. Though I didn't know it at the time, from the moment I was hit in the Hürtgen Forest, my entire life was set on a different course.

Betty and I got married in New Orleans on September 29, 1945—just weeks after Betty arrived home from France. George Stall, the paratrooper I'd become friends with in Stalag VII-A, and his wife, Fran, were there. I hadn't had time to sew my tech sergeant insignia onto my sleeve, so according to our wedding photo, I was just a staff sergeant. I didn't care much though. As far as I was concerned, with Betty by my side I felt like a three-star general.

We both lost people in the war. Betty's cousin Bob was a Navy pilot, and he never came back. Nobody knew what happened to him, which brought its own unique kind of pain to those who loved him. I had a friend from Columbus, a younger guy, who was killed in Europe. It could easily have been me.

But far more of our loved ones returned. Incredibly, all three of my brothers made it back. Carl served in India and Alaska, Glenn was awarded a bronze star for what he did in Guadalcanal, and Bud came back from Europe with a bronze as well as a silver star. Betty's brothers all served—and returned—as well.

Life was simple for us as we got settled in Columbus. We rented an apartment with the Stalls, and George's smile was even brighter now that he was back home. And when babies started coming along, we moved back in with Goffie for a time. Eventually the pull of the West Coast grew so strong we couldn't resist, and Betty and I made our home on the outskirts of Portland, near the same streets she used to play on as a girl.

From the beginning, Betty was a natural mother, and she raised all seven of our children with faithfulness, care, and love. She went back to nursing, but it took me longer to find a job that was the right fit. I was repossessing cars for one firm, but I stopped after a man pulled a gun on me.

"You need to put that away," I told him. "You don't know what I could do to you."

Eventually I settled into a job at the VA and took night classes at the local Bible school. For a time, Betty and I thought that we might become missionaries, but having seven children ruled out that idea for us. So we made a home and watched the family grow. We saw grandchildren and great-grandchildren come along, and eventually had enough Whipps kids around to field a couple of teams when we took a football to the park. It was only when I hit eighty-four that Betty finally put a stop to my playing running back. I didn't mind so much. By then Betty and I had been married so long we could hear the other's voice inside us just as loud as our own.

Some years ago, not long before the psychiatrist at the VA told me I was suffering from PTSD, another doctor told me I had something wrong with my heart. I always forget the name of the condition, but the way he explained it sounded kind of interesting to me.

"Your heart wall is enlarged," he said. "It means you're using your entire heart all the time, whereas other people don't have to."

I liked what he said. To use my whole heart seems to me to be a very good way to live. Not that I'm any kind of hero—I hope you know that by now. But I do know that if war taught me anything, it's that we hold back at our peril. In life, just as in war, there is much that could fill us with fear or cause us to retreat and observe from the sidelines. But I don't think life is meant to be lived that way. We aren't made to be timid, and we aren't made to withdraw when it comes to the things we give our hearts to.

The last thing Betty and I ever would have expected was that our story would be told in a book. Why would anyone want to read a story about two ordinary people like us? We didn't do anything that special. Other nurses were in far more danger, and other men acted with far more valor and received their rightful recognition. Besides, how many love stories do you know where the protagonists count each other's warts?

But we do know this: if it weren't for God, we would not have a story to tell. If not for God, we wouldn't be here together now. Everything we have is thanks to His love, His protection, and His gentle, behind-the-scenes guidance in ways we couldn't even begin to discern or understand at the time.

If you'll allow an old man a final moment to preach, I will leave you with this simple bit of advice—the best I have. Use your whole heart. Use all of it when you fall in love. Use every part of it to raise your family. Use all of it to trust God. Use it to be strong. Use it to be of good courage. Use it to fight fear. And use it to believe that wherever you are, God is with you.

Acknowledgments

Thank you to our dear Penny Whipps, who is responsible for this book being written. To our dear friend Craig Borlase, who has done an excellent job of writing. To Don and Brenda Jacobson and Marty Raz, who are all three wonderful friends, with special thanks to Don, who has been a super agent. To Carol Traver and the rest of the staff at Tyndale who have been amazingly helpful to us, with special thanks to the designer of the cover of the book. Thank you.

—Ray and Betty

By now, I hope that you feel as though you know Ray and Betty a little. I hope you love them a lot. They're every bit as wonderful as they seem, and I'm only sorry that this story doesn't do justice to their beauty, their love for each other, and their warmth. Sitting in their house, being fussed over at lunch, watching the way they still play and tease and dote on each other—these are some of my most precious memories. Ray, you are a man of honor, integrity, and humor, and I could listen to you pray for hours on end. Betty, you are kind, wise, and generous, and just the memory of your smile is enough to spark one of my own. Thank you both for taking a huge risk with me and for being the most wonderful authors to work with.

Summer 2013 was when I first heard about Ray and Betty, thanks to Don, my agent. Without his affection for them, his enthusiasm for crazy adventures, and his and Brenda's hospitality, this book would never have gotten off the ground. Thank you for all of the above and so much more. Brenda, it has been a pleasure getting to know you, and I am grateful for the multiple ways you have worked so hard to make me feel welcome in your home and to support this book. Don, you are more than an agent, and I thank you for being a friend, partner, and guru. This is not a bad way to begin, is it?

Marty Raz, as ever, you've been the glue, the eagle eyes, the hands and feet, and the voice of wisdom. Thank you for all this. Blair Jacobson, your skills have made this a better book, and I'm grateful to you for that.

This is the first, and most likely the only, book deal for which I have Twitter to thank. Even more thanks are due to the wonderful Carol Traver at Tyndale House for (a) tweeting about her experience of meeting World War II veterans, (b) reading my reply to her, and (c) taking a second look at the proposal for the book in your hands. Without Carol's courage, insight, guidance, and all-around brilliance, this book would be just another good idea gone stale. Carol, it's been a pleasure working with you, and if ever I go back on Twitter, I shall be sure to stalk you.

Stephanie Rische, I've never encountered an editor so encouraging as you, and I'm so grateful to you for your insight, your skill, and your hard work. Thank you, and I hope that this book makes you proud.

To the beautiful, charming, wise Emma Borlase, and the insightful Evie, curious Barney, wise-cracking Bessie, and cheeky Libby Borlase. Thank you for getting excited with me about Ray and Betty and for making it possible for me to go and spend time with them.

Lastly, I wrote every word of this book to a sound track supplied by John Williams, Michael Kamen, Gabriel Yared, and Yo-Yo Ma. I read each word out loud in my pretty abysmal Tom Hanks impression. Sorry, Tom.

—Craig

Bibliography

Blumenson, Martin. *The Patton Papers: 1940–1945*. Boston: Houghton Mifflin, 1974.

"First Battalion 22nd Infantry: Operations of the 22nd Inf Regiment in the Hürtgen Forest," accessed April 10, 2015, http://1-22infantry.org /history2/hurtgentitle.htm.

MacDonald, Charles B. *The Last Offensive*. Washington, DC: US Army Center of Military History, 1993. http://www.history.army.mil/html/books/007 /7-9-1/index.html.

Reeves, Robert D. "Life in Stalag VII A," Moosburg Online, last modified May 9, 2001, http://www.moosburg.org/info/stalag/ree5eng.html.

Rothbart, David. *A Soldier's Journal: With the 22nd Infantry Regiment in World War II*. New York: ibooks, Inc., 2003.

Ward, Geoffrey C., and Ken Burns. *The War: An Intimate History: 1941–1945*. New York: Knopf Doubleday, 2011.